From
Bitterness
to
RECONCILIATION

Learn to pull
out the roots
of bitterness
and find peace

From
Bitterness
to
RECONCILIATION

JAMES OFFUTT

SEL PUBLICATIONS
Syracuse, New York

I would like to dedicate this book to my wife, Connie,
who has been my faithful and supportive wife for 46 years.
Also, it is for all the men, women, and children
still suffering from the pain of bitterness.
My prayer is that they will find hope and help
from this book.

Acknowledgements

I want to thank my Lord and Savior Jesus Christ for showing me how unresolved anger can lead to bitterness in your life; the Holy Spirit for showing me the godly solution for this problem; and God the Father for His loving desire to have all of us reconciled back to Himself. I also want to thank my wife, Connie, for her ideas and encouragement, and to my editor, Tim Bennett, for his meaningful corrections and challenges concerning the text. In that regard, I also want to thank Ruth Cameron from Man in the Mirror Ministries for her helpful suggestions.

Contents

Introduction

This book had its genesis when I wrote my first book, *Anger Reconciliation*, which explores anger and conflict. During my research on anger, I encountered material describing the anguish of bitterness and its power to divide relationships. Since anger is the initial source of bitterness, it was natural for me to move onto bitterness and its various aspects for my second book. What surprised me was to find how pervasive bitterness is in our families and society in general. I learned of the extent of bitterness when I talked with the students at Syracuse Teen Challenge about their lives and families. Additionally, I encountered bitterness in Christians when I spoke at various churches on anger and conflict. What was even more surprising was how alarmed secular psychologists are becoming at the frequency of this problem in our society.

Personally, I experienced the pain of division caused by bitterness in my own family. My mother fought with her sister over a small amount of cash and a few personal trinkets that my great aunt had left to my aunt instead of my mother. This situation was very emotional to my mother as she had lived with and supported her aunt for seven years while her sister only supported her for three years. Consequently, after years of joyous family gatherings, all communication sadly disappeared forever in a sea of acrimony. My mother also never talked to her sister again as each waited for the other to give in and apologize. Regrettably neither forgave the other and my aunt didn't even come to my mother's funeral despite being told. I never met my cousin again as we lived in different states and she died prematurely. Sadly, I lost that opportunity for that relationship forever because of bitterness.

This book is broken up into three different sections. The first section, chapters 1-6 discusses what is bitterness, its sources, the steps leading to bitterness, and how fear may cause bitterness. The second section, chapters 7-10, talks about the importance of forgiveness, the steps to achieve forgiveness, the different reactions of the parties, and the aspiration for reconciliation with both parties. The last section, chapters 11-14, explores different types of conflict including conflict patterns ending up with positive conflict. Most people don't realize how negative conflict often leads people into bitterness. My goal is to help the reader understand bitterness, its deadly effect on us and our relationships, and to provide practical ways to overcome it.

The Holy Scriptures provide the foundational source for this book with all but four biblical quotes coming from the New International Version Bible and the others from The King James Version. I draw heavily from my 19 years on the staff at Syracuse Teen Challenge and from my experience of being a mentor to over 100 men during those years. Many of the students, ages 18-70, provide many of the stories in the book with their names changed to keep them confidential. The exception is, my former mentee and current friend, Junito Roman, who gave me permission to use his name in his story of being healed from the pain of sexual abuse. In addition to the stories from Teen Challenge I have also included stories from my life as well as men and women I have known to show how we all grapple with the pain of bitterness and conflict. They are placed in the book, without a lead in, to illustrate the proceeding principle that I have just discussed. I have also read over 25 books dealing with bitterness, fear, and conflict and have chosen appropriate quotes from them to draw attention to my points.

Bitterness is one of the least desired emotions, yet many of us end up there. This book seeks to provide bitter people with freedom from their prison of pain. My goal with the book is to help both men and women who have, knowingly or unknowingly, become bitter to find the peace that God offers.

When an angry conflict or threat occurs, there are initially at least two victims—the one that initiated the offensive action and the recipients of the attack. Often pride prevents reconciliation as each party waits for the other to apologize. If the wounds that originated the conflict or hurt are not healed quickly, the pain proceeds to poison one, or all parties, with bitterness. Then bitterness may infect those closest to each party as the verse in Hebrews 12:15 states: "*. . . that no bitter root grows up to cause trouble and defile many.*" It is my desire that this book will bring new hope of healing from these wounds and promote reconciliation to relationships fractured by bitterness.

One of my greatest aspirations for this book is to help pastors and Bible teachers to become more informed of the dangers of bitterness and the necessity to address this problem and give practical solutions for healing. Based on my experience of over 50 years in churches, I find that this issue is neglected from the pulpit, or in any other forum in a Christian's life. Consequently, people don't know what to do when bitterness has taken root in their lives. This book explains how we become bitter, how we can escape its clutches, and provides practical ways how we can stay inoculated from its poison.

— *Jim Offutt*

Chapter 1
What is Bitterness?

On the train to New London, Connecticut with my future bride, Connie, I was looking forward to meeting her parents for the very first time. I wanted to make a good impression on them because their daughter had, by this time, captured my heart. Just as we got off the train, a heavy rain began to soak us since we had no umbrella. Connie's father, a former career Navy Captain, met us also without an umbrella and directed us toward his car. By this point I was starting to feel water seeping through my shirt so I calmly suggested that we walk through the train station to avoid the drenching rain. Connie's father shot back, "How dare you defy my authority!" taking my suggestion as an affront to his leadership. He continued to yell at me unabated as we walked through the station to the car with his waiting wife. I was shocked into silence wondering if I had destroyed my opportunity for a possible marriage. Shortly after we started driving, Connie's father started screaming in an uncontrolled tirade against me. Everyone else in the car felt bludgeoned into silence for the remainder of the trip to the house. He left the house early the next morning and I didn't see him for the rest of my visit.

I felt deeply shocked at Connie's father's reaction. This was more than just anger. It was the first time I had experienced such intense bitterness. I learned from Connie that he would have these kinds of outbursts regularly alienating his children, and even his neighbors. Later, I discovered that he was caught in a generational conflict pattern of repeating what his father had done to him.

The definition of Connie's father's bitterness in *Webster's New Third International Dictionary* is "an intense or severe pain or suffering of mind . . . marked by animosity." (Note all future definitions will come from this dictionary). The Greek word for bitterness in the Bible is *pikria*. Rick Renner in his book, *Sparkling Gems from the Greek*, states *pikria* ". . . refers to *an inward attitude that is so bitter, it produces a scowl on one's face.* In other words, you become so inwardly *infected* with bitterness that you are outwardly *affected* in your appearance and disposition."

Bitterness is a powerful emotional condition that leads to the destruction of our most precious relationships. Paul warns us in Ephesians 4:31: *"Get rid of all bitterness, rage and anger, brawling and slander, along with every form of malice."* Paul is aware that a bitter attitude many times can result in the destruction of the person both physically and spiritually. Yet, bitterness has become so frequent in our society that some psychologists consider it to be a major heath problem and some even want it categorized as an illness. This view is supported in an article, *Bitterness: The Next Disorder.* by Christopher Lane in *Psychology Today* (May 28, 2009) "Bitterness is 'so common and so deeply destructive,' writes Shari Roan in the *Los Angeles Times*, ". . . that some psychiatrists are urging it be identified as a mental illness under the name post-traumatic embitterment disorder." In realty, no one ever starts out seeking to become bitter in their lives. In fact, if we told someone their words and actions were leading them to bitterness, they would probably deny it. Dr. Les Carter explains it like this in his book, *The Anger Trap:* "No one was born to become bitterly angry. Our Creator gave each of us life for the purpose of becoming both a recipient and a giver of love. Anger arises from the painful discovery that love is remiss, that judgment, rejection, or abandonment seems more sure." In summary, Dr. Carter is saying a lack of loving interaction in our relationships leads us to animosity.

Bitterness is a prolonged emotional state of unresolved anger reflecting a desire for revenge for some real, or perceived wrong. By not resolving or settling our anger, in effect, we have allowed Satan to come into our lives. Ephesians 4:26-27 (NIV) points this out scripturally: *"In your anger do not sin. Do not let the sun go down while you are still angry, and do not give the devil a foothold.*" Satan's foothold of unresolved anger starts us on the deadly path toward resentment and eventually bitterness (Note: we cover more thoroughly the steps leading to bitterness in Chapters 4 and 5). In his book, *Sparkling Gems from the Greek,* Rick Renner describes bitterness as "acid to one's soul that eventually begins to surface. When it does, the fruit it produces is *unkind, sour, sharp, sarcastic, scornful, cynical, mocking, contemptuous* and *wounding.*" Thus, it is so important to realize that every angry encounter has this toxic potential. My book, *Anger Reconciliation,* addresses biblical ways to express our anger and get positive results. In Chapter 7 of this book, I will discuss how we can be healed of the wounds that cause bitterness.

Bitterness is mainly caused by angry situations that occur in our lives that don't get resolved or forgiven. As a result the painful incident starts to consume our thoughts and feelings as we mull over the exact events of the angry conflict. In their book, *Overcoming Emotions that Destroy,* Chip Ingram and Becca Johnson discuss how anger should be temporary. *"It's okay to be angry—but it's not okay to befriend it. Anger is meant to be a passing acquaintance, not a longtime, live-in companion."* Yet we may tell ourselves, "Why can't the other person just understand my point of view and admit their fault. Then everything would be okay." Revenge against the perpetrator of our pain starts to control our daily thinking. This obsession may include devising malicious plans to hurt the other person with whatever options we have available to us. Our self-centered preoccupation with our pain gradually dominates our words and actions toward the original instigator. These actions take the form of withdrawal from any contact with the other person, speaking only to him/her in hostile ways, sending angry emails and/or telling others about the perpetrator. The thought is that I am hurting him/her through these actions and that is my way of making him/her feel my pain. With withdrawal, the instigator often doesn't feel the pain you would hope as they go on with their lives. Paul condemns these various actions as sin in Romans 12:19: *"Do not take revenge, my friends, but leave room for God's wrath, for it is written 'it is mine to avenge; I will repay,' says the Lord."*

THE EQUATION FOR BITTERNESS

Anger occurs → anger is unresolved and held in → offended party mulls over the painful events that caused the anger → resentment grows → bitterness develops → bitterness expressed → isolation occurs → physical & mental problems develop → bitterness becomes a way of life.

As we can see, anger develops because of a threat, frustration, unmet basic needs, hurt and/or violation of our values. The anger is not resolved because the angry person does not want to let go of the offense, or the offender refuses to take the steps for reconciliation. The offended party has the choice to forgive the offender, but instead holds onto his hurt feelings. This self-preoccupation continues daily so that the anger turns into resentment. Unless stopped there, the anger metastasizes into bitterness. Soon there is a desire to express the bitterness onto others. Because of the constant complaining, others leave the bitter person alone. The initial offense creates even more bitterness and physical and mental problems develop. These problems can even result in physical death, or leave the bitter person in a living death. If so, Satan has won a victory.

Summary:

1. Bitterness. Defined as an intense or severe pain or suffering of the mind and soul, an animosity.

2. It develops from unresolved anger. Unresolved anger is anger toward another person or situation that has not been worked out, or where forgiveness is not given.

3. Revenge. This develops in the mind and actions. Romans 12:19 says to let God do it.

Discussion Questions

1. What is your personal experience with bitterness in your family or relationships?

2. Are you experiencing bitterness now? If so, what are you doing about it?

3. Is someone bitter toward you now? How are you responding?

Chapter 2

Roots of Bitterness

The growth of bitterness in our hearts has been compared to how weeds develop. Once started, the roots of animosity go deep into our minds and psyche. Like weeds, bitterness is so difficult to remove once established. Hebrews 12:15 states: "*See to it that no one misses the grace of God and no bitter root grows up to cause trouble and defile many.*" Bitterness grows deep roots into your soul. You may remove part of the root but then the bitter feeling, like a weed, grows back again even stronger. For healing to be accomplished, there must be a complete removal of those deep roots from our lives. Also like weeds, bitterness can eventually take over your mind, heart and emotions just as weeds can overwhelm your yard. In that process, the good grass (healthy thoughts) are driven out as the weeds take over. Rick Renner in his book, *Sparkling Gems from the Greek,* describes the development of bitterness: ". . . bitterness doesn't overwhelm us all at once. Instead it grows a little here and a little there until it finally becomes a huge growth that defile our entire lives. Bitterness usually starts perking up out of the depths of our souls in the form of negative thoughts about another person."

There are several major roots that result in bitterness. They are as follows:

The bitter root of loss. This can be the loss of a close relationship caused by divorce, separation or the death of a family member. It is because the relationship was so dear to us, its loss hits us so deeply. That is when we often ask, "Why me?" Other painful experiences can be the loss of a job, a house to fire, or a car from an accident. Usually, however, the most excruciating losses are those that involve personal relationships because of the heavy emotional investment in them. To most of us, these relationships are valued as the most important parts of our lives.

Losing such cherished dear ones requires a time of grieving to help us adjust to a new life without that dear person. Job models a godly type of grief after he lost all his children. Job 1:20-21 states: *"At this, Job got up and tore his robe and shaved his head. Then he fell to the ground in worship and said: 'Naked I came from my mother's womb and naked I will depart. The Lord gave and the Lord has taken away; may the name of the Lord be praised.'"* In today's society, we don't tear our clothing or shave our heads to show our grief. Job's attitude of seeking the Lord in his grief, however, is what we need to do. We need to be patient because it will take time. He will heal our spirit as long as we persevere in holding Christ close to us in prayer. Usually it takes time for the grief process to be completed and acceptance is achieved. In the meantime, bitterness can easily creep into our thoughts as we express our sorrow. We think: Why now? Why did they leave me? What did I do to cause this? Why did God allow this to happen to me? We allow self-pity to take over our thoughts and emotions. Instead of seeking God in a deeper way, we blame Him for our situation. We become so consumed with our own painful condition that we turn to pain-numbing solutions like drugs, alcohol or sex.

Peter was married to Evelyn for 21 years and had two dear girls. They were both busy. Peter was successfully rising through the ranks at his corporation while Evelyn stayed home caring for their two daughters. She spent most of her time with them and tried to make their home welcoming to her husband, especially when he came home from work. Their marriage seemed to be working as both parties knew their respective roles.

Meanwhile, because of their mutual busyness, they had allowed their marriage to flounder. Slowly the relationship died in Peter's mind so he started seeing one of their mutual female friends. Then one day he told Evelyn he was leaving her and was getting married to their friend. Shocked to her core, Evelyn felt the pain of rejection and fear of loneliness. What would she do now? Anger, followed by bitterness, dominated her emotions. For days the tears flowed as she tried to get strength from her family and friends. Both her girls were out of the house in school so she felt so alone. She hated what Peter had done to her and also her former friend for betraying her. While Evelyn gained a good financial divorce settlement, she was constantly reminded of her pain when the two girls would split their time between the two parents for holidays. This feeling of loss continues in Evelyn's life today.

The bitter root of abuse. This involves the anguish of sexual, physical and verbal abuse. This root is particularly strong in a person's life. I have seen it in several cases at Syracuse Teen Challenge where I have been blessed to help men who were sexually abused. I realize that this abuse is even greater in women. These abuses, too many times, start at a young age and affect the person for the rest of their lives. Victims have told me how they have had serious problems hugging and feeling intimate with their loved ones. They feel like a wall comes up that stops their intimacy, even with their spouse. An underlying anger also springs up so powerfully in their lives that it often damages their closest relationships. Verbal abuse also leaves its scars in the form of fear controlling the person. Most abused victims develop a low self-esteem that affects their abilities to function in life. Too often they try using alcohol or drugs to dull the pain from their abuse. I was given permission from one victim to use the following true story of his sexual abuse and healing.

Junito grew up in the Puerto Rican section of New York City and was part of a gang, The Latin Kings. There he found a form of fellowship, but also danger and drugs. Hooked on crack, he started selling drugs to support his habit. After a time in jail, he sought a better life and came to Syracuse Teen Challenge (STC) as a wounded victim of early sexual abuse.

He was angry and rebellious, a sign of his pain from the abuse, so he left. He progressively became so depressed that he wanted to kill himself. Instead he decided to give God another chance and came back to STC with renewed commitment, but still suffering from the abuse.

I met with him regularly and he gradually began to trust me. I told him how I had helped other STC students successfully overcome the pain of sexual abuse using Theophastic Prayer, which is a nationally recognized healing ministry. The process starts with gaining the confidence of the hurting person enough to go to the painful events of the abuse. At that point, the facilitator asks the wounded person to bring their pain to Jesus and wait for Jesus to bring healing. During this time the facilitator prays to the Lord for healing. Some people receive words while others experience a feeling of peace. Junito. agreed to try it and, praise God, he was completely healed of his hurting memory. He now gives glory to God for a new freedom in his life. He successfully finished the Teen Challenge program and is headed for Bible school. His marriage is now much stronger and the bitter root is removed, thanks to Jesus.

The bitter roots of unfulfilled expectations. Expectations are defined by Webster's as "the state of looking forward . . . something that is expected." We all develop expectations for our relationships, jobs, lives and children. Robert Schuller discusses expectations in his book. *Leaning into God When Life Pushes You Away:* "We have expectations about the future—what it's going to look and taste and feel like. And when our expectations aren't met, we are let down. We're disappointed." Although this happens to all of us at sometime or another, the bitter person does not get over it. They have a feeling of loss which turns to anger and evolves into bitterness if it is not stopped. The different types of expectations are:

Expectations that are communicated. These are spoken and/or written expectations that we have for someone. We think we have told our spouses or children something we want from them, but they failed to do it for whatever reason. Consequently, we get angry when they don't meet that expectation. Then, we try to communicate our expectation again and the receiving person forgets it or blatantly disregards our request. Now anger is building up that can easily develop into bitterness. A helpful solution is to ask the person to use the **reflective listening** technique when communicating an expectation. This method is asking the receiving person to repeat back exactly what they thought they heard. If their response is not what you said, you repeat what you said and ask them to repeat again the process of telling you what they heard. While this process is somewhat time consuming, it reinforces your message and corrects misunderstanding, thus saving later frustration.

At Syracuse Teen Challenge, as with many other organizations, we require our students and staff to read and accept our rules of behavior and our procedures (expectations). We even have them sign a document stating that they have read and understood our rules. Thus, we are rightfully expecting these regulations to be followed and if they are not, we are justified in applying serious consequences.

Unspoken expectations. Those expectations that we believe the other person "should know" by virtue of our mutual beliefs or values. Dr. Dwight L. Carlson MD describes this expectation in his book *Overcoming Hurts and Anger:* "The reason for this could be that the person fears the disapproval of others or that it is difficult for the person to express his feelings. The expectations may not even be clearly enough defined in the person's mind to be expressed in words." Some men may lack the verbal skill to express their expectations so they may either hold back expressing their need or they express it poorly. The key is to at least try to express them so that the receiving person will have some idea of the request. Some examples of this include: a Christian expecting another Christian to act in a kindly way; a wife expecting her husband to take care of their children after she has had a long day home with them; and a boss expecting an employee to know his mind for some procedure when he is away. Most times such unspoken expectations are destined to be unfulfilled, which may result in anger and bitterness. Accusations may arise in the ensuing conflict like: "You should know what to do," "You are thoughtless and I can't trust you with anything." Such comments only incite more anger escalating into animosity. To avoid such conflict, we need to spend the needed time to properly prepare people by explaining clearly our expectations, and even writing our expectations down.

Unknown expectations. These are those expectations that we don't even know yet but will be coming up. These arise from change(s) in our lives like a husband or wife losing their job, creating new financial stress on the family.

It could be an accident that injures one of the family requiring hospitalization and the subsequent necessary visits. Such change(s) place a whole new set of expectations and stress on all of us. We can't completely prepare for such events. However, we can take steps to minimize the effects of such sudden change: by obtaining proper insurance, setting aside financial reserves, developing contingency plans for emergencies and thereby reducing the stress if the unexpected occurs. Such stress on people, already under stress, can easily lead to tension and conflict possibly ending up in bitterness.

Some ways to reduce stress are: getting sufficient sleep, family prayer, a healthy diet, setting aside time to talk to each other and developing cooperation among family members.

Then, we have the healthy resources to meet the challenges of such unexpected events.

Some people develop unreasonable expectations, which they will boldly express as "their rights." Examples of such unreasonable expectations include: the government supplying everyone's needs, a teacher giving only A's on all their tests, and requiring perfect cleanliness from someone. Such unreasonable expectations usually create frustration leading to anger. As a result, all expectations need to be measured through the lens of practicality. If the expectation fails this test, it needs to be confronted and a revision made.

Another danger with expectations is when they are expressed as demands. Because we feel such an urgency for the other person to do our wishes, we use strong demanding words to convey our need. In their book *Overcoming Emotions that Destroy*, Chip Ingram and Becca Johnson state: "Watch out when you find yourself using such words as *ought, should, must, always* and *never*." The authors go on to say: "These words can be reliable indicators that our expectations may have been transformed into demands." Such demands are often met with anger from the receiving person since those words are used as an exaggeration to make a point and are rarely the truth.

Because expectations are so prominent in our lives, when major expectations are not met we often times blame God. After all, he is supposed to be in charge and "We haven't done anything to deserve this." Yet, what we fail to recognize is God may have allowed this to happen to us for our own good. He has a better plan as Robert Schuller explains in his book, *Leaning into God When Life is Pushing You Away*. Schuller writes: "Discover who God made you to be and learn to conform your expectations to the kinds of things God seems to bless. And don't compare how God meets someone else's expectations with how he meets yours. His plan for your life is unique." So we need to seek out our own special gifts and ask for God's direction on how to use them for His glory. Then, our deepest expectations will be met.

The bitter root of rejection. Rejection is defined by Webster's Dictionary as "refusing to acknowledge, adopt, believe, acquiesce in, receive or submit to." The pain of rejection happens to us all, but it is especially devastating when it is done by someone close to us. We are wired to look for acceptance and love in all our relationships. This, however, is not realistic or possible because others will reject us for making mistakes or for just being different. The anguish of rejection from a spouse or friend can be so severe that people may do damage to themselves or to others when trying to alleviate it. Accordingly, we are in turmoil within ourselves but we can't get rid of it without the Lord's help.

Robert Schuller points out in his book, "But human rejection happens and we still feel the pain. And to compound matters, we often feel that others' rejection is our fault." Schuller rightfully points out that blaming ourselves is not a positive solution. Later in his book Schuller explains that the best solution for rejection is coming to God. "If you have been shattered by the pain of rejection, you must let God be the artisan of your soul. You must embrace the conviction that your shattering is not the end of something beautiful. And you must wait patiently to see what God will do. Don't be quick to assume that God is finished. Give Him time to pick up the pieces and begin to craft something new and beautiful in your life." Too often, we become impatient with God and we try to take control and resolve the situation ourselves. Such action will often fail since we don't seek God's directions. Our role is to stay connected to God daily and to listen for His direction.

Laura had grown up with Philip on Nantucket Island. For years they had played together and had become friends. In their teens, Laura developed a crush on Philip who did not return her feelings. Later he dated her occasionally, but didn't seem that interested in her as he went out with other girls. Eventually, however, he started seriously dating her, which filled her heart with joy. They got engaged and Laura dreamed of the day when they would marry. It seemed perfect to her but Phillip had some doubts about marrying her. Just before the scheduled wedding, Phillip abruptly broke off the engagement. Laura's pain of rejection was profound. For days she brooded in silent despair. A root feeling of deep bitterness gradually took control of her heart towards Philip for how he had hurt her with his fickleness.

Philip went on with his life in New York City unaware of Laura's bitter feelings toward him. As Phillip grew older and his friends were getting married, however, he realized that he too wanted to get married. Thinking back, he remembered all the good times he had had with Laura. He started to call her and they started to date again. Within only several months, Philip asked her to marry him. She agreed and the wedding was held.

The color of the bridesmaids' dresses was noticeably somber. They left on the honeymoon only to return after one day. Apparently, Laura had rejected Philip on their wedding night and the marriage was never consummated. Laura's revenge had now been complete. Now it was Philip's turn to taste the pain of bitterness. They divorced shortly thereafter.

The bitter root of ill health. This occurs when we become injured in some unexpected way, for a long-term period or possibly for life. This situation is particularly poignant when someone is young and the injury affects their entire lives. Joni Eareckson Tada became a quadriplegic for life at age 17 from a diving accident. In her book, *A Lifetime of Wisdom,* Joni cries out from her pain from such a change in her life: "God . . . do you bring people into this world to just breathe, eat, grow old, and die? Do You toss the dice and paralyze people, or throw in a little cancer . . . a little Down syndrome?" She explains in the book how she found a reason to live by serving and encouraging others with physical handicaps, which eventually became an international ministry.

Even in the latter stages of life when our bodies start to break down, we can begin to resent these physical and mental challenges coming into our lives. We try to help our bodies stay healthy through better diets and more exercise, but in reality we are wasting away. Paul comments on this in 2 Corinthians 4:16: *"Therefore we do not lose heart. Though outwardly we are wasting away, yet inwardly we are being renewed day by day."* No matter our age or physical condition, ill health can turn us into sour, bitter people if we allow it. Our only hope is to seek God to help us to manage these changes and develop in us a positive attitude while we are alive on this earth. The way we can do this is by believing in the truth of the Bible, which says we will have new bodies in heaven for all eternity.

The following shows the various ways bitterness can enter our lives:

Bitter Root of Loss/Suffering
Bitter Root of Abuse
Bitter Root of Expectations:
  Communicated, Unspoken & Unknown
Bitter Root of Rejection
Bitter Root of Ill Health

Any one of these can start us on the path to bitterness.

When we develop one or more of these bitter roots, we have a feeling of grief. Webster's defines grief as: "an emotional suffering caused by bereavement, affliction, remorse, panic, and despair." These emotions are deeply expressed in the Bible in Job 3:25-26: *"What I feared has come upon me; what I dreaded has happened to me. I have no peace, no quietness; I have no rest, but only turmoil."* Elizabeth Levang PhD in her book, *When Men Grieve,* discusses the turmoil in our lives: "Grief creates a sense of chaos. It destroys our connection with the familiar, patterned, and comfortable reality. It robs us of our dreams and cheats us out of our future. What was has ended." Also in Job 7:11: *"Therefore I will not keep silent; I will speak out in my anguish of my spirit, I will complain in the bitterness of my soul."* We see here is deep emotion expressed for a personal loss that can lead to bitterness. This type of anguish can be good for us as it helps us to release some of the pain. Dr. Elizabeth

Kubler-Ross, in her ground-breaking book on grief from death, *On Death and Dying*, amplifies how this expression of grief is very important. "Let the relative talk, cry or scream if necessary. Let them share and ventilate." She states later: "Some, often men, hold in this open expression of sorrow as 'unmanly', but it will come out eventually in some other possibly self-destructive way such as using drugs, alcohol, or sex."

Additionally, often anger is held against the person who hurt us, even after that person has died. This expression of anger is really part of a grief process that we all go through in our own way. In her book, Dr. Elizabeth Kubler-Ross outlines five stages of grief: Stage One: Denial and Isolation; Stage Two: Anger; Stage Three: Bargaining, Stage Four: Depression and Stage Five Acceptance. She explains how anger is a part of the grief process: "The process of grief always includes some qualities of anger." Such anger is part of the adjustment to the change(s) that are occurring in our life from the loss. The degree of our loss through death, divorce or rejection by loved ones is always the strongest loss.

We all would like to move quickly through these stages to "acceptance," but the grief process requires time and can't be rushed for the healing process to work. Each person grieves in his/her own personal way because a personal loss(s) has taken place. There has been an important change in our lives that will affect how we live going forward. Elizabeth Levang PhD in her book, *When Men Grieve*, explains how grief brings change to our lives: "Grief is the steward of change. The many choices and decisions we face in our grief will undeniably alter our life path. Our world has changed, externally and internally. There is no going back, no way to recapture the past. We are in a wretched state of uncertainty." Such uncertainty often brings feelings of fear and anxiety because we don't know the full ramifications of such a change. We don't like these feelings so anger often comes out at those around us, and even at God. Yet seeking God in this grief process is the help we truly need as He knows our every thought and feeling. He will eventually give us the solace we so desperately seek. If we trust Him and are patient, He will guide us through the restoration process.

Summary:

1. Roots of Bitterness. Develops from very painful situations. Some are:

> **a. The bitter root of loss.** This includes death, divorce or loss of relationship with a loved one. It is probably the most hurting of the various bitter roots.

> **b. The bitter root of unfulfilled expectations.** We all look forward to ways members of our families will meet our needs. Also we have expectations for our jobs, our families, and our lives. The types are:

>> **1) Expectations that are communicated.** These are the ones we know.

>> **2) Expectations that are not communicated.** These we know but have not been communicated or understood by others.

>> **3) Expectations that are unknown.** These we don't know yet but are percolating up to be either communicated or uncommunicated expectations.

> **c. The bitter root of rejection.** When others reject us or our values and ideas. This can be caused either by our actions or those of others.

> **d. The bitter root of ill health.** Can happen to us, at any age, usually not because of our own habits but can be (smoking, drinking, excessive eating, and using drugs).

These bitter roots can develop into bitterness when we nurture the hurting feelings that arise in us. We let those agonizing feelings dominate our thoughts.

We feel grief. Defined as an intense mental sorrow when these bitter roots develop in us. Anger is a part of the grieving process.

Discussion Questions

1. Have you experienced any of the roots of bitterness?
If so, what happened?

2. Explain the three types of expectations.

3. Understanding the problems with these expectations, what will
you do differently?

4. Were you able to grieve after any loss in your life
(i.e. death, divorce, injury etc.)?

Chapter 3

Biblical Examples of Bitterness and Other Characteristics

Unresolved animosity is seen in the lives of several biblical characters. Michal, David's first wife, is a striking example. Samuel 6:16 states: *"As the ark of the Lord was entering the City of David, Michal daughter of Saul watched from the window. And when she saw King David leaping and dancing before the Lord, she despised him in her heart."* We see the roots of bitterness starting to take hold in Michal. First, she didn't have the same close relationship with God as David did, or even that of her brother Jonathan. Secondly, she probably held lingering resentment over how her father Saul had treated her. He had given her to David to be his wife, taken her from David and given her to Paltiel and now had given her back to David. Thus, there may have been fertile soil in her heart for her resentment to bubble to the surface when she saw David's joy in dancing for the Lord.

Additionally, David exposing most of his body embarrassed her. These feelings are vividly expressed in verse 6:20: *"When David returned home to bless his household, Michal daughter of Saul came out to meet him and said, 'How the king of Israel has distinguished himself today, disrobing in the sight of slave girls of his servants as any vulgar fellow would.'"* The painful consequence she received from God for her hostile outburst is described in verse 6:23: *"And Michal the daughter of Saul had no children to the day of her death."* In those times in Israel, not being able to have children was considered to be a curse from God, so her childlessness must have resulted in great pain in Michal's life. Also, we don't read anything more about her relationship with David after this incident as he apparently spent his time with his other wives. As a result, Michal appears to have lived a very lonely life during her later years. The lesson for us all is that unresolved anger has deadly consequences: sometimes far greater than the original hurt. We need to learn to resolve our anger through forgiveness and asking God to help us work out our angry situations.

Continuing the metaphor of comparing weeds to bitterness from the last chapter, we see that weeds tend to spread as their seeds travel in the wind in our yard and even to our neighbor's yard. Bitterness is the same as it starts to infect those around us, especially our family. Our friends may become enveloped by a web of animosity that keeps on infecting people—even to the point of affecting whole churches, communities and nations. Hitler's bitterness poisoned a whole nation against the Jews before and during WW II. The same can be said of Haman in the book of Esther. Chapter 3:5 reads: *"When Haman saw that Mordecai would not kneel down or pay him honor, he was enraged. Yet having learned who Mordecai's people were, he scorned the idea of killing only Mordecai. Instead Haman looked for a way to destroy all Mordecai's people, the Jews, throughout the whole kingdom of Xerxes."* Haman found a way to kill all the Jews in the kingdom. We see how quickly the flame of revenge that Haman had for Mordecai quickly became a forest fire extending to others who were not even involved in the original incident. Thus, a bitter attitude toward one person can quickly become prejudice toward an entire race.

Next we see the infection of bitterness extending to Haman's family and friends in verses 5:10-14: *"Calling together his friends and Zeresh, his wife, Haman boasted to tell them about his vast wealth, his many sons, and all the ways the king had honored him . . . . 'But all this gives me no satisfaction as long as I see Mordecai sitting at the king's gate.' His wife Zeresh and his friends said to him, 'Have a gallows built . . . to have Mordecai hanged on it.'"* Now Haman's family and friends become involved in his plot of revenge by aiding him with their advice. Effectively the lethal web has expanded drawing in those around Haman. In the end, they too reap the deadly cost of such vengeance. We too can suffer the same consequences when we are drawn in by our family's bitterness. Verses 7:8-9 tells of the penalty of Haman's bitterness: *"So they hanged Haman on the gallows he had prepared for*

Mordecai . . . ." His family too was seriously harmed in verses 9:9-10: *"They also killed . . . the ten sons of Haman . . ."* As we see, seeking bitter revenge results in devastation to our families and spreads even wider to include friends and neighbors. Bitterness is one of Satan's most potent tools to destroy us and those around us. Consequently, we must seek ways to heal the sources of our anger reasonably quickly.

OTHER CHARACTERISTICS OF BITTERNESS

Often bitter people like to express how they have been misunderstood or maligned. They justify their deep anger so as to gain sympathy from friends and build allies that will side with them. Their goal is to gain more allies than the other person in the conflict. This action makes them feel right and confident in their stand. Those who don't agree with their complaints are pushed away and are considered like enemies. Meanwhile, the bitter person continues to nurse his/her grudge against the offended person by the gathering of like-minded allies. This action gives the bitter person a false illusion of power, which he relishes. Eventually, however, the acrimony starts to destroy these allied relationships so that the person ends up alone, bitter and misunderstood. Such a state results in the person feeling even more animosity and so the downward path continues for him/her.

Other characteristics of a bitter person are marked by: frequent conflicts with other people, critical attitudes towards others, sarcasm and a form of self-righteousness. These negative actions create in us a sour personality that is repulsive to others. Chris Brauns in his book, *Unpacking Forgiveness,* relates to this sour attitude: "We all know sour people who kick dogs, yell at children cutting through yards, and shout at church business meetings about insignificant issues. They are cynical at work." Also, we develop a critical attitude that is negative about our lives. Such a pervasive, pessimistic attitude soon spreads to the world around us as everything seems depressing. The glass is always "half empty" as we fail to grasp the positive things happening in our lives. Consequently, we become unforgiving and judgmental towards others. We remember every little detail about the original painful event and others' actions and become preoccupied in self-pity. In their book, *From Anger to Intimacy,* Gary Smalley and Ted Cunningham write: "Replaying anger is like gossip. We tend to make up the details that didn't actually happen, and by doing so we can even begin to develop negative beliefs." Later they continue: "When we rehearse the scripts of fights in our minds, we have a tendency to overlook important details and see things that are not there." In our anger we develop biased memories that bolster our own opinions that miss the truth thereby creating an unrealistic thinking. Just the rehearsing of the many details of a painful event in our lives demonstrates that we are probably harboring bitterness.

THE PHYSICAL & MENTAL EFFECTS OF ANGER & BITTERNESS

The emotion of anger physically unleashes the following as Gary Oliver describes in his Book, *Real Men:* "Physiologically anger triggers an outpouring of adrenaline and other stress hormones to our central and peripheral nervous systems with noticeable physical consequences. Your voice may change to a higher pitch. The rate and depth of your breathing increases. Your perspiration increases. Your heart beats faster and harder. The muscles of your arms and legs may tighten up. The digestive process is slowed down." We all can recognize these physical symptoms in ourselves when we get angry. All these physical effects are from the immediate feeling of anger, but can be reduced if we would stop and pray to calm down and get God's help.

The physical effects of unresolved anger (bitterness) are similar to anger but different as portrayed by Chip Ingram and Becca Johnson in their book, *Overcoming Emotions that Destroy.* "Unresolved anger can also destroy us *physically* as we internalize feelings. We develop intestinal problems, muscle strain, ulcers, colitis, and headaches, among other maladies. We become more easily fatigued and stressed. When our anger level is high, our physical and emotional tolerance level is low." These physical effects are magnified when we hold in our anger. Many people think that stuffing their anger will cause it to dissipate. The truth is the opposite since anger is energy that must eventually be released. Meanwhile anger is destroying us on the inside. As Gary Oliver reveals in his book, *Real Men*: "A person who stays angry and hostile—even long after the particular incident that caused the anger—may be committing slow suicide. Charles Cole, a Colorado State University psychologist, suggests that the physiological effects of the mismanagement of anger and other emotions may cause blood vessels to constrict, increased heart rate and blood pressure, and eventually lead to the destruction of the heart muscle." Thus, for our physical lives, we must effectively resolve our anger.

The mental effects of unresolved anger include: a cynical and hypercritical attitude and can even lead to mental illness. This is supported by the article on bitterness on the web by *An Independent Baptist Church* (www.gospelcenterchurch.org/bitterness). "I wonder how many people with mental breakdowns, depression, manic-depressive, bi-polar, and all types of such problems, could be traced back to unresolved bitterness and hurt over past experiences that has caused the person to harbor bitterness." Accordingly, we must learn to resolve our anger before our own mental health is in danger.

In the next chapter we shall see how any of us can unknowingly go through the steps from anger to bitterness.

Summary:

1. Biblical examples of bitterness. The story of Michal and David show the devastating effects of unresolved anger in Michal's life. Also, Haman in the book of Esther demonstrates the destructiveness of bitterness to: Haman, his family and his friends.

2. Other aspects of bitterness: person justifies his bitterness to himself and others. He seeks allies only to lose them eventually. Also he has a cynical attitude that dwells on replaying the details of the conflict.

3. Physical effects of bitterness. They are: heart problems, stomach problems, headaches and muscle problems.

4. Mental problems of bitterness. They are: critical attitude, constant worry and even mental illness.

Discussion Questions

1. What was the real source of bitterness for Michal and Haman?

2. Name three of the physical or mental effects, of bitterness?

3. Have you experienced any of the other characteristics listed in the chapter?

4. Have you ever experienced any physical/ mental effects of bitterness?

Chapter 4

Stages One and Two
of Bitterness

Bitterness develops in us through various stages. However, if the pain is very intense, it can move rapidly from anger to bitterness. If the animosity develops gradually, we have the choice at each stage to end it there before it moves onto the more dangerous stage—bitterness. These stages are as follows:

Stage 1 Unresolved anger. Anger occurs when we first feel fear, frustration, an injustice, or hurt to us by someone. Anger is our reaction to that initial feeling. When we are hurting, we want to change what has happened to us so usually we react negatively in some way—either aggressively, passive-aggressively, or by holding in the anger. For a more complete explanation of all types of anger expressions see my book, *Anger Reconciliation,* Chapters 2 and 3. The intensity of our anger is usually increased directly by how close we are with the other person.

When our anger is not resolved in some way through reconciliation, forgiveness, or compromise, we unknowingly start down the path toward bitterness. Scripturally, we have allowed Satan to gain a foothold as stated in Ephesians 4:26-27: *"In your anger do not sin. Do no let the sun go down while you are still angry and do not give the devil a foothold."* Through his foothold in our minds, Satan causes us to feel the pain and concentrate our thoughts on our anger. As Chip Ingram and Becca Johnson state in their book, *Overcoming Emotions That Destroy:* "Opening the door to the destructive power of anger—even just a little—invites a terrible, potentially terminal monster to reside in our hearts." If we realize the necessity to resolve the anger now before Satan takes control of our minds and spirit, we can avoid the much greater pain in the later stages. The conflict becomes more destructive, not only to us, but those around us.

I have drawn on Rick Renner's internet article, adding my own additions, on unforgiveness leading to bitterness. Rick explores this connection in Luke 17:6 (King James version is used below and on the next page). In that verse, Jesus tells His disciples: *"If ye had faith as a grain of mustard seed, ye might say unto this sycamine tree . . ."* Jesus chooses to use the analogy of the sycamine tree with unforgiveness or bitterness. This tree is significant as Rick Renner points out in *Sparkling Gems from the Greek:* "No wonder Jesus used this tree as an example of bitterness and unforgiveness! Like the sycamine tree, bitterness and unforgiveness must be dealt with clear to the roots, or they will keep springing up again and again. The roots of bitterness and unforgiveness go down deep into the human soul, fed by any offense that lies hidden in the soil of the heart." Rick goes on to say "It will take a serious decision for that person to rip those roots of bitterness out of his heart once and for all . . . ." It is remarkable to realize that the significant similarities between bitterness and the sycamine tree. They are:

1. **Both have deep roots.** In fact the sycamine tree has some of the deepest roots of any tree in the world. Unforgiveness keeps growing deep into our hearts and lives, so it is hard to pull it out. Also, if bitterness, like the tree, is cut at only the surface level, it springs back to life again. To eradicate animosity completely, we have to cut the roots down deep or they will regenerate.

2. **The fruit of both is bitter.** The sycamine tree produces a fruit, a fig, that is very bitter to eat; just like the bitter fruit of unforgiveness: hostility, unfriendliness and envy.

3. **Both are pollinated by being stung.** The sycamine tree must have its fruit stung by a wasp to pollinate while bitter people feel stung by the hurt inflicted by the other person. Often bitter people will express: "I will never let that person sting me again."

4. Both grow very quickly in dry environments. The sycamine tree is known in the middle east as probably the fastest growing tree in an arid climate. Bitterness is also known to flourish very quickly in the hearts and minds of spiritually dry people where there is a lack of forgiveness and repentance. Bitterness, like the tree, will takeover whole areas of our lives and even whole communities.

5. Both will bury you. The sycamine wood is most often used to make caskets in the middle east because of its easy availability and its quick growth. Bitterness, once in full bloom, will bury you physically, emotionally and spiritually.

As we read Luke 17:3-4, we see the importance of forgiveness. Here Jesus is trying to teach his disciples about the need to forgive: *"Take heed to yourselves: If thy brother trespass against thee, rebuke him; and if he repent, forgive him. And if he trespass against thee seven times in a day, and seven times in a day turn again to thee, saying, I repent: thou shall forgive him."* Jesus is stressing the importance of us granting forgiveness not just once, but repeatedly. He is trying to help His apostles and us to avoid the danger of unforgiveness because He knows that it will end in the prison of bitterness. Jesus continues the lesson in verses 17:5-6: *"And the apostles said unto the Lord, 'Increase our faith.' And the Lord said,' If ye had faith as a mustard seed, ye might say unto this sycamine tree, Be thou plucked up by the root, and be thou planted in the sea; and it should obey you.'"* Thus, if we even have little faith, we too can dispose of our bitterness into the sea. Sadly, too often we don't exercise our faith in Christ but instead keep the bitterness inside of us.

To illustrate each stage, we will be using a true story of how a deep friendship between two close friends started with simple anger, then step-by-step evolved into bitterness. The names have been changed, but you will see a true portrait of the anguish of unresolved anger. Such could become true for any of us.

Will and Joe had been friends since they were children. While Will was two years older than Joe, they had played together since their earliest days. They held a common interest in sports and seemed to bond together in so many ways that they became almost like brothers. As they grew up, married and had children, their close connectedness continued as they both were baseball coaches for their children's teams.

One day Will met with Joe to tell him he was furious with him for endangering his son, Dave, with his reckless driving from the last baseball game. According to Dave, Joe, in his intensity to get to the game on time, was speeding excessively and driving so dangerously that he had sideswiped another car. In the anxiety over his son's safety, Will heatedly asked Joe, "What were you thinking by driving so dangerously with my son in the car?" Shocked at Will's passion, Joe explained that he was driving only five miles over the speed limit. Furthermore, he hadn't hit any car and that Dave was lying. The word "lying" set Will off into an angry tirade. Will then angrily told Joe in a harsh voice that, "You will never drive my son again." Also, Will wanted Joe to apologize to Dave for saying that he lied. "Until you do these things, we have nothing more to talk about and our relationship is dead for now."

All this caught Joe by such surprise that at first he remained silent. Then he replied claiming innocence but soon cruel words poured from Joe's mouth. This action ignited a more heated conflict as neither party would back down, or try to understand the other. It seemed as though the years of close relationship were slipping away. They each left the conflict unresolved with each other smarting from the painful exchange.

In effect, Will and Joe had started down the path described at the beginning of Ephesians 4:26: "*In your anger do not sin . . .*" Their anger wasn't wrong, but the way they expressed it was sinning with their disrespectful words and harsh tones. Since the way we express anger is a choice, Will had better options. He never really tried to understand Joe's side, but totally believed his son. Joe also reacted to this callous treatment by sinning with his response. He could have reduced the temperature of the conflict with a calmer voice and showed respect even when it wasn't shown to him. In their book, *Overcoming Emotions that Destroy,* Chip Ingram and Becca Johnson point out the damage of unresolved anger. They state "Unresolved anger breaks relationships, allows Satan a foothold . . . ." In effect, a forest fire had been started between these two close friends as described in James 3:5-6: "*Likewise the tongue is a small part of the body, but makes great boasts. Consider what a great forest is set on fire by a small spark. The tongue also is a fire*" Neither party considered dousing the flames of negative anger with forgiveness. This action could have probably stopped the conflict at this point. Instead, the disagreement escalated into the festering stage.

Stage 2 Festering on the anger. Festering in this way is defined as "a progressive irritation or malignancy-rankle (an injustice that will fester in their minds until the situation is corrected)." People who are at this stage dwell frequently on the unresolved conflict, mulling over what the other person said and did, and why it was so wrong. The exact details are remembered of what was done to them and they rehearse them constantly. Gradually they become preoccupied with their angry emotion(s), feeling that an injustice was done to them. In effect, the emotions have taken over the person and a bitter spirit is developing in their heart. They fail to recognize any part they had in the conflict because they have a sense of self-righteousness. Moreover, they will probably discuss their angry feelings with family members to gain allies in their battle. They do not bring their problem to God except to ask God to change the other person. As a result, they violate the intent of verse 4:26 of Ephesians: ". . . *Do not let the sun go down while you are still angry.*"

This stage also involves the emotion of fretting or worrying about how the conflict will end. Fretting, in the sense used here, is defined as "the action of eroding: a wasting away or being wasted away as if gnawed or eaten." If you are in this phase, you feel that you are being eaten up with your angry emotions and wonder how you can find your "rightful justice." Psalm 37:8 discusses this fretting state: *"Refrain from anger turn from wrath; do not fret—leads only to evil. For evil men will be cut off, but those who hope in the Lord will inherit the land."* When angry situations start to consume our thoughts regularly, we need to be aware of the danger of bitterness coming into our lives. Chris Bruns reinforces this point in his book, *Unpacking Forgiveness:* "When we have been deeply offended, we may find ourselves thinking over and over about what happened. We mentally run in place. The more we think about it, the faster our thoughts go, and the faster our thoughts go *nowhere."* In effect, Chris Bruns says it is like we are on a mental gerbil wheel, running as fast as we can but going nowhere. This consuming feeling within us, with no end in sight, can quickly lead to depression. Instead of descending into this vortex, however, we need to consciously turn to God for help and solace. He will slow down our mind and give us peace in time.

Unfortunately, Will continued to mull over on the details of his angry confrontation with Joe. He replayed every word spoken and his anger toward Joe festered more each day. He would say to himself, "I am just protecting my son and that is the most important thing." Will discussed these feelings with his wife, who immediately supported him since she never really liked Joe anyway. In addition, he elicited the support of his children, which he thought he got. Now he felt more justified in his stand.

Still Will felt a sense that something important was being lost in his life—his close relationship with Joe. They formerly would see each other frequently and have fun together. He could safely unburden his troubles and concerns with Joe and not feel condemned. There was truly a unique nature to their relationship, which Will didn't have with any other man. Now that special relationship was broken and he missed it. Thus, he had many ambivalent feelings going on. Still he had to support his son. Will kept telling himself that he had to stand by his position even if the friendship went away. Will held out the hope that Joe would also miss their relationship and seek his forgiveness. Only this action, he thought, would bring peace to the conflict.

As the days went by, there were no calls or any other communication from Joe. Hope of a resolution seemed to fade when Joe didn't call and admit his fault. Will did not consult the Bible or seek God for spiritual help with his emotions. Every night Will stayed awake being consumed with reviewing the details of the conflict and each of Joe's stinging words. Will felt as though his life was being devoured with the pain of the injustice done to him and his son. His sleepless nights were often spent in mental turmoil.

Gary Chapman highlights what is happening to Will in his book, *Anger: Handling a Powerful Emotion in a Healthy Way*. He writes: "In the person's mind, the initial scene of wrongdoing is played over and over like a videotape. He sees the other person's facial expression; hears the person's words; he senses his spirit; he relives the events that stimulated the angry emotions. He replays the psychological audiotapes of his own analysis of the situation." Paul in I Corinthians 13:5 speaks against this: *"Love is . . . not easily angered, it keeps no record of wrongs."* Thus, we see Will spiraling into stage three—resentment.

Summary:
Stages of Bitterness

1. Stage 1 Unresolved Anger. An angry conflict that is not resolved to the satisfaction of both parties can lead to one or both of the parties starting down the path towards bitterness (Ephesians 4:26-27). The intensity of the feelings is directly related to how close the offender is to us. Each party has a **choice** to continue to hold on to the hurt, or forgive the other.

2. Stage 2 Festering. Defined as "a progressive irritation or malignancy-rankle." (Psalm 37:8). People in this stage demonstrate the following:

a. Develop a self-preoccupation with the details of the conflict, especially the words and actions of the offender.

b. Feel the injustice of the wrong done to him. They develop a self-righteous attitude. They do not bring their problem to God.

c. Start to fret or worry about how the conflict will end. This becomes an endless action going nowhere and not resolving the conflict.

Discussion Questions

1. Have you felt unresolved anger toward someone in your family? What happened when you tried to resolve this disagreement?

2. Have you brought your conflicts to God in prayer for Him to show you what to say and do?

If not, why not? If you did, what happened?

3. Are you now spending long amounts of time mulling over how and what someone did to hurt you?

Chapter 5
Stages Three and Four of Bitterness

Stage three, resentment, continues the downward progression leading to step four, bitterness. The remaining two stages are as follows:

Stage 3 Resentment develops. Resentment is defined as "a feeling of indignant displeasure because of something regarded as a wrong, insult or other injury." Job addresses resentment in Job 5:2: "*Resentment kills a fool and envy slays the simple.*" Because of the sense of injustice from the injury, the person allows evil thinking to develop in his mind. In effect, Satan has gained a foothold as described in Eph.4:27, and is using it to control the person's thought patterns for sinful actions like revenge. The Bible speaks against revenge in Romans 12:19: "*Do not take revenge, my friends, but leave room for God's wrath, for it is written 'It is mine to avenge; I will repay, says the Lord.'*" Too many times we, in the intensity of our anger, take over the correction that God would perform much better than ourselves. In so doing we are sinning.

One of the common ways of revenge, even in Christian circles, is to go into a "hostile silence" mode toward the offender, his family and friends. This means not talking or communicating in any way with the offender and his/her allies. The person starting this payback thinks that he will punish the offender with no interaction. Then, he too can feel some pain. Ironically, the opposite often occurs as the offender goes on with his/her life except he becomes aware of this avoidance tactic. Gary Chapman in his book, *Anger: Handling a Powerful Emotion in a Healthy Way*, discusses the danger of "hostile silence." "This 'silent treatment,' the withdrawal and avoidance, may last for a day or for years. The longer it continues, the more certain it is that resentment and bitterness will grow and fester."

Another characteristic of resentful people is a very critical attitude toward those around the offender. When they look around, they feel like the world seems to be against them and there is little that is positive. They become sarcastic or demeaning about the offender, and all the past positives of their relationship are forgotten. An attitude of sarcasm, cynicism and hostility is projected onto others, which frequently causes them to withdraw from the relationship. Accordingly, this action creates even more resentment. A barrier to emotional growth develops, which is manifested by a lack of trust in others and a loss of confidence.

I continue the story of Will and Joe from the last chapter.

Will was now expressing his anger about Joe to everyone around. He knew in his mind that Joe was wrong and he wanted everyone to agree with him. When that didn't happen he started to shun or employ "hostile silence" with those who opposed him, particularly Joe's friends. Even within their mutual friends there was an ambivalence of whom to support. Several didn't want to take sides but tried to remain friends with both. This dual support infuriated Will who felt more betrayed and withheld communication from them. Will's loneliness closed in on him as everything seemed dark.

Meanwhile, Will's level of hostility grew stronger because of another source. His daughter, Sandy, who initially supported Will and her brother, Dave, changed her mind as she became jealous of all the attention her brother was receiving because of the incident. Will would attack his daughter for her increasing hostility to him and her lack of support for himself and Dave. What complicated the situation was that Sandy had happily played with Joe's daughter for several years and they had become close friends. Consequently, Sandy started acting out in rebellious ways. There was a heightened tension pervading Will's household marked by sharp words between Will and his wife.

Progressively, Will's world seemed to close down on him as feelings of despair took over. Joe still didn't call to apologize. His family, friends and even God seemed to be deserting him in his time of need. Will had been saved but had only a lukewarm faith. In his despair, he cried out to God: "Why is this happening to me? I didn't do anything wrong! It's all Joe's fault, punish him." But there was no answer: it seemed as if God wasn't there.

Despair is defined as "utter loss of hope: complete domination by feelings of hopelessness, futility or defeat." We see Will's surrounding relationships deteriorating such that despair starts to devour him. In her book, *When Men Grieve*, Elizabeth Levang, PhD states: ". . . despair is marked by a slow descent into an emotional prison." Later she writes: "Attempts to rationalize the situation fail, and life increasingly slips out of control." Finally she states: "Despair directs men away from hope and toward self-destruction." Unfortunately, Will was headed for a depression and even more serious problems.

Finally, Will's resentful attitude became a barrier to connecting with God because he was sinning by maintaining and not resolving his anger. We, too, can fall into similar sin with our anger so that we can't connect with God. When resentment has taken over their hearts, even strong Christians who have been regularly attending church will stop going, discontinue reading their Bibles, and even stop praying. It appears to them that God is of no help, so God and religious faith is diminished severely. God wants them to seek help through forgiveness of the offender, but they choose not to do so.

Valery Satterwhite in her internet article, *Resentment and Expectations: Big Fat Hold Ups* points out the devastation of resentment. "Resentment is a thief that you invite in to steal your personal power. The more you resent the more you feel victimized and powerless." Will had allowed this victimized feeling to take over his life. His resentment had now descended into bitterness. As Jim Wilson highlights in his book, *How to be Free from Bitterness:* "Someone gets hurt and he gets resentful. Resentment turns into deep bitterness. Bitterness is just resentment that has been held on to. It has become rancid and rotten. It is kept in and it gets worse."

Stage 4 Bitterness. We defined bitterness earlier as "an intense or severe suffering of the mind." This definition reflects how our mind is under great agony, which starts to affect other parts of our body, particularly the heart. Ezekiel conveys a powerful word picture in verse 36:26 about how God can overcome the bitterness that can infect the human heart. *"I will give you a new heart and put a new spirit in you; I will remove from you your heart of stone and give you a heart of flesh."*

Each stage of bitterness hardens our hearts of flesh (sensitive compassionate hearts) into a heart of stone which is self-centered, cynical and hostile. This deterioration is due to Satan's continuing control of our thoughts and lives. We seldom recognize our descent into bitterness because of our preoccupation with the hurt from the other person. Most of us unknowingly allow this decline to continue even though we have a choice at any stage to end it by forgiving the person.

The story of Naomi in the Old Testament book of Ruth testifies how bitterness can take over. The untimely deaths of her husband and her two sons caused Naomi to feel bitter. In Ruth 1:20, Naomi says: *"'Don't call me Naomi,' she told them, 'Call me Mara, because the Almighty has made my life very bitter. I went away full, but the Lord has brought me back empty. Why call me Naomi? The lord has afflicted me; the Almighty has brought misfortune upon me.'"* We can feel anguish in her voice over her status as a widow without the financial and relational support of her husband, or her two sons. Undoubtedly, she also felt the fears of loneliness and probable starvation creeping in since widows in those times frequently lived in poverty. Naomi, like many of us when we reach this stage, blame God for our troubles. Like all trials, this was a testing of Naomi's faith in God, which is common for most bitter people. God, however, showed her His grace by giving her a loyal companion, Ruth. Later, He rescued Naomi from her destitute state by arranging for Ruth to marry the wealthy Boaz. and thereby provide for

Naomi financially. It was Naomi who blessed Ruth by introducing her to God.

Bitterness is based on believing someone hurt you, either true or imagined. It is possible to misunderstand someone's conversation or actions resulting in unresolved anger leading to animosity. Jim Miller, in his book, *How to be Free from Bitterness,* states the bitter person believes the offender is guilty. "Incidentally, many bitter people cannot imagine the possibility that they are bitter over imaginary sins. As far as bitterness is concerned, the other person's guilt is always real. For such a person trying to be free from bitterness, it is acceptable for them to assume the real guilt of the other person, *so long as they get rid of their own bitterness.*"

This principle states: how close we are in our relationship with the offender, the greater the potential for love or acrimony. There is an expectation for resolution of our anger that starts with the family, expands out to close friends and extends to our church family. Most Christians have low expectations for non-Christians to want to resolve conflicts but much greater expectations for Christians for the same. Initial animosity can easily develop into generational bitterness, which I will discuss later in the book.

Soon Will was finding new grudges at others in his immediate world. His boss did not recognize his long, hard work on a project in the way Will had expected. His wife's affection mysteriously disappeared. Will's former friends stopped calling him. A pervasive sense of loneliness began settling into his spirit. Will felt anger at all of them, but he also needed them. He was in a dilemma for which he knew no answer. In his self-preoccupation, he ended up more withdrawn and hopeless as ever.

His continuing hatred of Joe had not helped Will to feel any better as he had expected. "Why wasn't Joe feeling guilty for what he had done and said?" "He was the one who had committed the wrong!" "Where was God's justice?" Soon,

Will began questioning whether God was even there or even cared about him. As a result of his doubt in God, he stayed away from church and reading his Bible. Will also started to get headaches and his sleepless nights continued as an overall depression crept into his life. As a result of these physical problems, his work performance plummeted, causing him to take a leave of absence from his job. Why was he suffering so much? Will's life had become a consuming turmoil.

Gwen Mouliert points out Will's condition in her book, *Overcoming Bitterness:* "Bitterness and resentment will shut you into a prison where even your most desperate questions and prayers seem to fall on deaf ears. This is far worse than any physical condition could be." As a result of the length and depth of Will's animosity, his heart and spiritual condition were being controlled by Satan who wanted to destroy him. Gwen Mourliert goes on to describe the effect on his spirit: "What exactly is anguish of the spirit? Try 'intense turmoil.' When bitter roots have begun to grow, we experience a great deal of inner turmoil. Sometimes that brings the sort of confusion where we can't really define what we're feeling, but we know there is a problem deep inside us." This is the place where Will was emotionally.

Another important characteristic of bitterness that may develop in us is a spirit of envy, which defined means "painful or resentful awareness of an advantage enjoyed by another, accompanied by a desire to possess the same advantage." When we develop enmity in our lives, we may also exhibit the same jealousy of others who seem to be in better situations. Such is shown in the story of Simon the Sorcerer starting in Acts 8:9: *"Now for some time a man named Simon had practiced sorcery in the city and amazed all the people of Samaria."* The story continues in Acts 8:14-23. *"When the apostles in Jerusalem heard that Samaria had accepted the word of the God, they sent Peter and John to them. When they arrived, they prayed for them and that they might receive the Holy Spirit, because the Holy Spirit had not yet come upon any of them; they had simply been baptized into the name of the Lord*

Jesus. Then Peter and John placed their hands on them, and they received the Holy Spirit.

"When Simon saw that the Spirit was given at the laying on of the apostles hands, he offered them money and said, 'Give me also this ability so that everyone on whom I lay my hands may receive the Holy Spirit.' Peter answered: 'May your money parish with you, because you have thought you could buy the gift of God with money! You have no part or share in this ministry because your heart is not right before God. Repent of this wickedness and pray to, the Lord. Perhaps he will forgive you for such a thought in your heart. For I see that you are full of bitterness and captive to sin.'

"Then Simon answered, 'Pray to the Lord for me so that nothing you have said may happen to me.'" We see how envy had crept into Simon's heart as he wanted the power of the Holy Spirit for himself. Peter rightly rebukes him for his sin and points out his problem. Then Simon appears to admit his mistake and asks for repentance. When we are struggling with anger we often start envying others who have apparently better lives. Satan will use jealousy to further destroy our mental health.

As a hurt person, we feel justified in our initial anger as it is **all** the offending person's fault. As we progress through the various stages leading to bitterness, we continue to maintain that justification so that it takes on a pridefulness. Erwin Lutzer in his book, *When You've Been Wronged: Moving from Bitterness to Forgiveness,* writes this "What the bitter, offended person is saying is this: 'My hurt is so deep, the offense done to me is so great that nothing I do can be as bad as what is done to me.' All hope of seeing himself for what he is, has vanished. He denies his bitterness when he can and justifies it when pointed out."

By holding onto his anger, Will is sinning, as is Joe, so that in reality we have two sinners. Will chose not to forgive and in so doing, his spiritual life deteriorated because of his continuing sin. In fact, his bitterness could easily become an idol that he worships daily instead of God. Erwin Lutzer goes on to say: "Clearly his relationship with god is optional; his need for immediate vengeance is not. Thus, his bitterness, like ours, can become an obsessive idol of the heart." In so doing, we are committing the sin of idolatry, which violates God's Ten Commandments Exodus 20:3: "*You shall have no other gods before me*" and Exodus 20:4: "*You shall not make yourself an idol.*" As a result, Satan has us worshiping the wrong god, which he knows will lead us away from the very help we need in the one true God.

We have seen the steps leading to bitterness starting out with an angry conflict that remains unresolved. We all have the opportunity to choose to forgive or continue down this destructive path. In fact, we can stop the descent at any time by choosing to forgive and/or trying to resolve the situation. Usually, we don't recognize our own sin when we are committing it. Consequently, we need to ask God to help us recognize our sin, confess it and forgive the offender. Then God can heal our pain. We will have followed Paul's sage advice in Ephesians 4:31-32: "*Get rid of all bitterness . . . . Be kind and compassionate to one another, forgiving each other, just as in Christ God forgave you.*" God also knows the sin committed by the offender and He will bring justice to him in His own way.

We will discuss more in Chapter Seven Intentional Forgiveness Leading to Reconciliation.

Summary:
Stages three and four of Bitterness:

1. Stage 3 Resentment. Defined as "a feeling of indignant displeasure because of something regarded as wrong, insult or other injury." A resentful person shows the following:

> a. Evil thoughts toward the offender in their mind. Allows Satan to gain a foothold in his mind Eph.4:27. Seeking revenge violates Romans12:19. Leave room for God's wrath.
>
> b. Withdraws from the offender and his allies using "hostile silence." Develops a lack of trust in others and loss of personal confidence.

c. Develops a critical sarcastic attitude toward those around him/her causing others to stop relating. This action leaves the person more isolated.

2. Stage 4 Bitterness. Defined as "an intense or severe suffering of the mind." An example is Naomi in verse 1:20 from the book of Ruth.

a. Bitterness can develop from real or imagined hurts. The bitter person becomes preoccupied with the hurt of the other person. The other person's guilt always seems so real.

b. Bitterness is like a prison—trapped and closed in—feeling intense inner turmoil.

c. Develops envy—"painful or resentful awareness of an advantage enjoyed by another . . ." Simon the Sorcerer in Acts 8:9.

d. Continuing to hold onto bitterness becomes a sin—can also become and idol.

Discussion Questions

1. Do you feel like withdrawing in "hostile silence" from someone who has offended you? What other godly action could you take"

2. Are you aware that you are sinning by holding onto your anger at someone? How could you stop this sin?

3. Has bitterness started to develop in your family? What steps can you take to stop it?

Chapter 6

Fear Leading to Bitterness

I purposely have included this chapter on fear as I know from both personal experience plus my experience of 20 years with students at Syracuse Teen Challenge that fear is a major cause of anger. I have found students trapped by their negative fear(s) often lashing out in anger, which if unresolved or unforgiven, turns into bitterness. Most people don't realize this connection to bitterness. Consequently, you will see how paralyzing fear is a true danger in our lives.

We all have experienced some form of fear during our lifetime. Nevertheless, fear comes into our lives in several forms such as reverence to God, self-awareness of danger, to a paralyzing fear that holds us in bondage. For this chapter, we will only be focusing on the paralyzing fear that debilitates us. Webster's defines this particular type of fear as: "an unpleasant emotional state characterized by anticipation of pain or great distress accompanied by heightened autonomic activity." This form of negative fear sets off a powerful emotion that controls our actions and thereby our lives. Such an apprehension is designed to alert us to what we believe, in truth or in falsehood, is a danger to us. Thom Rutledge in his book, *Embracing Fear,* talks on this aspect: "Fear is an alarm system. It is there to get our attention, to push us in one direction or another, out of harm's way." The Bible addresses this particular fear in Proverbs 29:25: "*Fear of man will prove to be a snare, but whoever trusts in the Lord is kept safe.*" This verse contrasts the fear (reverence) of God vs. the fear of other humans, who will judge us. Because we want to please others, we inadvertently get caught in the deadly trap of becoming "people pleasers." In any case, we are not seeking to become trapped.

What are the origins of this negative trepidation in us? Most fears develop in childhood where the world seems very frightening: everybody and everything is bigger, darkness is so scary, and we are faced with new terrifying experiences that can affect us for life.

When I was young, I went to the doctor for shots, which is normal for any young child. In reality, the shot is only a momentary sting and hurts only for a moment. Yet, the way that doctor inserted those needles left such a lasting painful impression on me that I still, to this day, strongly fear needles. This phobia was further fortified when I was sick with a cancerous tumor in my lymph system. The doctor needed to insert a large needle into my arm for the marking dye to see my lymph system on a screen. A new resident, doing the procedure, was so intent in inserting the needle into my arm that he failed to heed my cry to "Slow down, I have a real problem with needles." The whole procedure was cut short, when I suddenly went into shock. I remember the feeling of fear made me very angry at the young resident for not listening to me and putting me through this painful trial. This example shows how fear can lead to anger resulting in bitterness.

In my early years, I went to the dentist to remove some cavities. The dentist told me, with encouraging words, that I could face the pain of the drilling without any Novocain. With his gentle, yet persuasive manner, I learned to withstand the pain of drilling. Today, I go the dentist and tell him not to give me Novocain, unless absolutely necessary. I firmly believe the quick shot is worse than minutes of drilling.

I fully realize that the above story doesn't make any logical sense, but that is the peculiar nature of fear in our lives. Because our experiences vary individually, our fears are also very irrational in nature. This peculiar feature of fear is portrayed by Jeff Golliher in his book, *Moving Through Fear and Finding the Courage to Live Your Life:* "Why is this peculiar? Because whether we realize it or not, we're afraid of one thing or another nearly all the time. I have to conclude that we make very little headway in differentiating between true (objective) fears and false (baseless) fears." Our painful experiences, that leave a lasting scar on our psyche, will determine our main fears. These experiences can include: divorce, death of a loved one, loss of a job, and breakup of a close relationship. I have friends who have felt such pain from their divorce that they hold a bitter spirit in their hearts against their spouse who hurt them. Several of them even fear remarriage to avoid possible future anguish.

Another origin of our fears is believing what others tell us, whether it is true or not. When young, we tend to look to our parents or authority figures for wisdom and guidance, but they are sometimes confused and lead us astray. I have had students at Teen Challenge (between the ages are 18 to 60 with an average age of probably 30) tell me how their parents, who were drug addicts themselves, introduced them to drugs.

What we perceive as any threat to our emotions or relationships can start us on the path toward a new fear. Thom Rutledge explores this topic in, *Embracing Fear:* "Every difficult emotion we experience represents some kind of threat—a threat to our self- esteem or to the stability of a relationship (personal or professional), even to our right to be alive." These threats appear so strong in our minds that we allow them to control our lives so that we lose our focus and even become bitter about our lives. The irony is that there are new threats that we have not yet encountered that potentially may cause us to develop new fears. Consequently, our world of fears is constantly in flux.

The power that fear has in our lives comes from our own thoughts and beliefs. Too many times our beliefs are based on a lie. Consequently, we can easily act in hurtful ways to ourselves and others. Jeff Golliher discusses this point in his book: "Fear can close our hearts, shape our emotional life, and freeze our attention, but the only power that fear has is the power we give it." We, in effect, have the ability, if we want, to control the strength of negative fear. Regrettably, we often give into our fears and allow them to control our thinking and existence. As fearful people, we start to constantly rehearse the particular fear in our minds, which becomes a daily ritual. Often we become frustrated with the fear, which in turn becomes anger, and eventually bitterness. This action causes us to turn our focus away from our real problems. To find quick solutions, we mistakenly look for worldly answers, instead of God. Unfortunately, many of us start using and depending upon drugs, alcohol and/or pills as a medication for our fear. Paul provides us with a biblical answer in Romans 12:2: "*Do not conform any longer to the pattern of this world, but be transformed by the renewing of your mind. Then you will be able to test and approve what God's will is—his good, pleasing and perfect will.*"

The various components of debilitating fear are as follows:

Anxiety. Defined as "an abnormal and overwhelming sense of apprehension of fear marked by such physical symptoms as tension, tremor, sweating, palpitation, and increased pulse rate." We all have had moments of anxiety when a threat may seem intense to us at that time. Harold S. Kushner in his book, *Conquering Fear,* quotes Margaret Miles of Harvard University, who described the physical effects of anxiety: "'Anxiety is the number one health problem in the country leading to epidemic depression, alcoholism, eating disorders, and prescription drug addiction . . .'" Thus, we see how physically dangerous anxiety can be.

> Susan had just received the good news that she had been accepted to teach first grade at a nearby school next fall. This event was a dream come true as she had gone to graduate school to get her teaching certificate, and had been an assistant at the school for several years. Yet, despite this positive experience, the weight of responsibility suddenly hit her. Was she up to the task? Would the children like her? These and other questions flooded her mind and life with anxiety.
>
> All summer her sleep was restless and her daytime was spent wrestling with her doubts of her ability to meet this new challenge. Tears, tension and anger flowed throughout the house that whole three months. It was as if she had forgotten

the years of being a confident, capable assistant. Her anxiety turned to anger at her husband who tried to calm her fears. He told her "I know you will succeed as a teacher. You have good experience and love the kids." But she did not believe it. Lacking the strength of knowing and trusting Jesus with her anxiety, the summer became joyless as Susan grappled with her doubts. She was consumed by her anxiety and striking out at those dearest to her.

With the advent of fall, she began teaching and all her past experience and education kicked in; soon she felt the joy of excelling. All her anxiety had been a lie and the truth was: she was a natural teacher. She went on to teach many years and was greatly appreciated by her students and the administration.

This true example shows how lies lead to anxiety that can preoccupy us, and affect those closest to us. The weight of anxiety is expressed in Proverbs 12:25: *"An anxious heart weighs a man down, but a kind word cheers him up."* This anxiety becomes so powerful, that it causes us to live in terrible bondage. Sadly, we often fail to recognize the truth of the situation and get rid of the lie(s). Therefore, we may live in a constant state of fear. Paul admonishes us in Philippians 4:6-7: *"Do not be anxious about anything, but in everything, by prayer and petition, with thanksgiving, present your requests to God. And the peace of God which passes all understanding will guard your hearts and your minds in Christ Jesus."* Paul knows that when we truly turn to Jesus with our apprehension, God will bless us with true peace from the turmoil of Satan's anxiety, which can easily start us on the path to bitterness.

Dread. Defined as "an extreme fear-inspired reluctance to face or meet a particular person or situation." We all have felt dread when we are forced to meet an authority figure who we know will be judgmental of us. Our senses are heightened, as we try to put forth our best selves. Inside of ourselves, our hearts are pounding and our stomachs are churning. Miriam sings about dread in her song in Exodus 15:15-16:

"The chiefs of Edom will be terrified, the leaders of Moab will be seized with trembling, the people of Canaan will melt away; terror and dread will fall upon them." We see in this verse how dread and terror are linked, which often is the case in our lives.

Worry. Defined as "mentally troubled or concerned . . . constrict, to press." In Luke 12:22-23, we see Jesus giving his disciples a warning about worrying: *"Then Jesus said to his disciples: 'Therefore I tell you, do not worry about your life, what will you eat; or about your body, what will you war. Life is more than food and the body more than clothes.'"* Later in verses 12:25-26: *"Who of you by worrying can add a single hour to his life? Since you cannot do this very little thing why do you worry about the rest?"* When we worry we become too concerned about ourselves and forget about God and others. Other negative aspects of worry are: it ruins our health, consumes our thoughts, keeps us in bondage, and we lose productivity in work.

Being worried about someone or something is not the same as having concern for the same situation. When we worry, we are in effect paralyzed into inaction and preoccupied with the problem or threat. Conversely, with concern, we turn to God to help us focus on developing plans and actions to deal with the problem. Consequently, we follow Luke 12:31: *"But seek his kingdom and these things will be given to you as well."*

Phobia. Is defined as "an exaggerated and often disabling fear." A phobia is a relentless fear of an object or situation that is disproportional to the actual danger involved. Its emotional force is so powerful that it often controls our life. In, *Real Men*, Gary Oliver PhD depicts phobia: "When someone has a phobia, his fear is out of proportion to the situation. It is beyond voluntary control; it cannot be reasoned or explained away. He knows his fear is unrealistic but he can't seem to stop it. People who are phobic live on the edge of panic." Some examples of phobias are: acrophobia—fear of heights, agoraphobia—fear of public places, aviophobia—fear of flying, cardiophobia—fear of the heart attack, and even philophobia—fear of falling in love, or being in love. In fact, there are so many types of fears that there is at least one for every letter in the alphabet, except q and x. I suffer from acrophobia. For example, when I went to the top of the Eiffel Tower in Paris, I felt compelled to stay as far from the railing of the observation deck as possible. With time, however, I found that I gradually gained the courage to approach the railing, but never reached it. This experience has been repeated countless times throughout my life, but I have gradually become less fearful of heights.

Such phobias can make us angry at our circumstances that make us so fearful. Sometimes this anger gets directed towards God: "Why did you make me with this phobia or fear?" "God why won't you take this away from me?" Then when God doesn't heal us, we get bitter at God.

Fright or panic. Defined as "terror excited by sudden danger." Fright is a short-term intense fear that quickly arises in us from a grave threat. We become frightened when we unexpectedly encounter something, or someone, that we feel is dangerous to us. Panic alerts the body's system to go into a self-protective mode so that adrenalin starts pumping through our veins and into our muscles. Such bodily preparation enables us to gain amazing physical strength and alertness.

One hot day, when my son was about two, we decided to take him to a beach at a nearby park. I was to watch him for a few moments while my wife was busy with something. As my son and I were holding hands walking along the beach front, I met my secretary from work and we started talking. Suddenly, I realized that my son had pulled his hand out of mine and had left me. I could feel the panic surge throughout my body as I frantically ran along the beach front. I called to my wife, "Andrew's left me! Help me look for him, now!" As she joined me we raced along together looking and calling out for him. At that moment, the adults were performing a human chain across the lake looking for some poor missing person. My heart went into my throat, as I thought it might be for my one and only child.

Finally, we came to the shelter for the lake and found him sitting on a box calmly looking around. Apparently, a life guard had found him and set him there. In any event, the panic had destroyed the rest of our afternoon.

The degree of panic is related to the importance of the missing person, event, or the magnitude of the danger involved. When panic hits us, additional fears pile up as Jeff Golliher explains in his book, *Moving Through Fear and Finding the Courage to Live Your Life:* "Whatever the physical causes of panic may or may not be, its the unpredictable nature of the "attack" that makes them scary. Often our response is to add one fear on top of another, the panic makes us susceptible to additional fear." As a result, when panic hits us, we develop a hopeless feeling, causing us to think of the worst outcome(s). This process can lead to depression where all hope seems to have left us. We lack God's strong peaceful assurance. A helpful biblical example of panic is in Exodus 14:10-11: *"As Pharaoh approached, the Israelites looked up, and there were the Egyptians marching after them. They were terrified and cried out to the Lord. They said to Moses, 'Was it because there were no graves in Egypt that you brought us to the desert to die?'"* Soon after in verses 4:13-14 we read: *"Moses answered the people, 'Do not be afraid. Stand firm and you will see the deliverance the Lord will bring you today. The Egyptians you see today you will never see again. The Lord will fight for you; you need only to be still.'"* As we later discover, the Lord opened up a path through the Red Sea where the Israelites safely passed through on dry ground, while the following Egyptians were drowned by the Lord's hand.

Terrified. This fear is the most debilitating of all of them in that it imprisons us from taking action. It originates when we encounter extreme danger to ourselves that could easily lead to our death, such as: being on the front lines in a war, or being in an airplane falling to the ground, or falling off a high cliff. At these times our minds and bodies may freeze because of the terror we feel. Jeff Golliher calls this point the abyss: "This fear goes well beyond the experience of panic. The feeling is of a 'place' within us that might open to the so-called bottomless pit. It's not that the familiar world is no longer reliable or that we are losing confidence in ourselves. The sense here is that the world we know *within ourselves* and regard as structured, relatively secure, and meaningful seems to vanish." This vanishing means we have lost our familiar sources of strength that we struggle to hold on to. Consequently, we feel totally lost emotionally. Maybe that is how the saying "There are no atheists in foxholes!" originated. Finding a connection with God in these crisis situations gives us the supernatural strength, that we are so desperately lacking and for which we are truly searching.

All these components of immobilizing fear may develop in us sequentially (i.e. we may start worrying about something, which evolves into anxiety and in turn into panic). This process may happen slowly or quickly depending on the importance of who and what is involved. Other times, we go straight to panic mode. As we have seen from the components of fear, Satan uses them to imprison us in constant chaos. In this paralyzed state, Satan wounds us physically, emotionally and most importantly spiritually. We lose hope of any relief and anger arises often ending in bitterness.

Steps to overcome fear. The following are the steps using biblical principles:

1. Acknowledge that you are controlled by fear. Realizing that you are allowing fear to take over your emotions and thinking. Fear, like a coward, tries to stay hidden in the darkness and stay unrevealed. Fear doesn't like to be brought out into the light of day as fear lives in denial and evasiveness. Facing our fears and seeking help allows us to start to unlock the prison that we have created for ourselves.

2. Pray to God about your fear. Bring your fear(s) to the Lord for new strength and direction and He will help you to overcome them. As Isaiah 41:10 states, *"So do not fear, for I am with you; do not be dismayed for I am your God. I will strengthen you and help you; I will uphold you with my righteous hand."* He will help calm your fears and anxiety as 1 Peter 5:7 comforts us with: *"Cast all your anxiety on him because he cares for you."* In effect, we turn over our fears to the Lord and He will give us new confidence, peace, and direction on how to deal with them that will work.

3. Determine if lies are controlling you. Satan uses our fears against us by ensnaring us to believe his lies. As John 8:44 points out *". . . He was a murderer from the beginning, not holding onto the truth, for there is no truth in him. When he lies, he speaks his native language, for he is a liar and the father of lies."* Lies can cause us anxiety and even panic, thinking that all is lost. In effect, it destroys our hope. This is why we must turn to Jesus for the truth as He will reveal to us any lie(s) behind our fears. Then we can walk and live in the truth as John 8:32 states: *"'. . . If you hold unto my teaching, you are my disciples. Then you will know the truth and the truth will set you free."* By realizing the truth, we now know how to take corrective action to reduce our fear(s).

4. Read and memorize Holy Scripture. When we feel fearful the Bible can provide the inspiration and direction we need to diminish our fears. As the verse in Psalm 119:105 proclaims: *"Your word is a lamp unto my feet and a lamp for my path."* As we read this verse, we see that the Bible provides a light for us to find our direction when we are lost in the turmoil of fear. It is only as the light of the Word, penetrates the darkness of fear that surrounds us that we are delivered from our fear(s). One such powerful verse to help us overcome fear is Isaiah 35:4: *"say to those with fearful hearts, 'Be strong, do not fear, your God will come, he will come with vengeance; with divine retribution he will come and save you.'"* And Psalm 27:1: *"The Lord is my light and my salvation—whom shall I fear? The Lord is the stronghold of my life—of whom shall I be afraid?"* These and other verses encourage us during our times of fear. The Psalms are particularly effective when feeling fear, as they express and help us to sort out our emotions. His Word brings us closer to Him.

5. We seek His presence. Connecting with Jesus at our time of fear brings peace to the torment in our lives. This step applies, even when we are facing death from some illness or threat. By seeking to relate directly with Jesus, we discover His wisdom and guidance for us. Psalm 16:11 reinforces this: *"You have made known to me the path of life; you will fill me with the joy in your presence, with eternal pleasures at your right hand."* Also in James 4:8: *"Come near to God and he will come near to you."* His presence brings a joy, yet a calming to our storm of fears. We feel that, no matter what happens, we will be all right. Whether we live or die, we have a peaceful place to go, because Jesus will be with us.

When I was 31 and just married two years, I encountered unrelenting pain in both knees. I ended up going to the hospital for a week of tests, which showed nothing. My job had me scheduled to go to Caracas, Venezuela for a two month stay. So it appeared that I was going. Fortunately, a friend who was a nurse, expressed her alarm at my situation and told me to get another opinion. When I went to the second doctor, he told me to get into the hospital immediately, which I did.

There, I was given tests by the doctors to find out about the pain in my knees. Finally, they saw something on an x-ray and decided to perform exploratory surgery in my chest. There they found a large cancerous tumor. They did not remove it, as they thought that in so doing, they would spread the cancer. So they closed me up and scheduled me for experimental x-ray radiation treatments. The doctors told my wife, not me, that they expected me to live for only two months. When my wife told me this, I immediately felt fear flood my emotions and then anger: "God, why was this happening to me now? I don't deserve this!" After spending some days sorting out my emotions, I realize that I was in a life or death struggle. As a result, I sought greater strength for myself so I asked her for a Bible. While we had gone to a church regularly, it was not a Bible-believing church. Even though I had never read much of it, nor was I "saved," somehow I knew that it could provide the spiritual strength that I needed for this desperate time.

In the subsequent days, my emotions ranged from anger at God to feelings of despair. Everyday, I kept reading the New Testament. Gradually, my hopelessness started to leave me, as I gained hope in Christ. I started feeling like Jesus was talking to me and I began to feel His presence for the first time in my life. I told Him "Jesus, I surrender my life to you. I know that if it is Your will that I die, You have a wonderful place for me to go, heaven." A new confidence in my future filled my heart and mind. Shortly thereafter, as I was sleeping, I saw this brilliant light flood the room and fill me with a soothing peace that overwhelmed me. My fear was replaced with new hope.

6. Faith in God replaces fear. Fear has us dwelling on our negative feelings and problems while faith gives us hope by thinking of the positives in our lives. Through our faith we know that, even if we die, we will be with Jesus. Realizing this fact, we elect to exchange our fear for the stronger faith in Christ and His principles. As 2 Timothy 1:7 states: *"For God did not give us a spirit of timidity, but a spirit of power, of love, and of self-discipline."* Thus, Satan's power over us, using our fear(s), is gone; now our hearts find new peace. We have faced our greatest fear and overcome it by trusting Christ completely with our lives. We have a new confidence to face the many threats in our lives. Then, He can now guide us and bless us. My story continues.

My physical condition remained the same despite the x-ray treatments and their accompanying burns on my neck. Then, two weeks after my encounter with Christ, the doctors tested me and found no cancer. The doctors couldn't believe it.

Then they predicted that I would not live more than five years. Christ has now kept me alive for over 40 more years. I'm so grateful that the doctor's prediction was wrong. Faith in God is our answer to conquering fear. Praise God!

Fear is one of the most powerful forces in our lives. Fortunately, Christ's power is greater, as long as we access Him when we encounter fear, or its components. Now when I face fearful threats, I always recall that time Christ saved me from certain death. This inspiring memory diminishes my fear. While you may not have faced death yourself, you probably can remember a powerful testimony of how Christ brought you, or someone else, through some danger or deathlike experience. When we recall such powerful memories, they are the inspiration to help us overcome Satan in our battle with debilitating fear. The Apostle Paul reminds us about how God calms our fears in 2 Corinthians 7:5-6: *"For when we came to Macedonia, this body of ours had no rest, but we were harassed at every turn—conflicts on the outside, fears within. But God, who comforts the downcast, comforted us . . ."* As we know from later verses, Paul did not let fears stop his ministry, but Paul proceeded onward. We too should adopt that same persistent attitude in our lives.

Summary:

1. All have experienced some form of fear. There are different types of fear. This chapter's focus is solely on paralyzing fear, which is defined as: "an unpleasant emotional state characterized by anticipation of pain or great distress accompanied by heightened autonomic activity." This fear controls our actions and sets off an alarm (Proverbs 29:25).

2. Most fears develop in childhood where the world seems frightening. Our painful experiences determine our main fears. Also believing lies others tell us. Any threat to our emotions can start a new fear.

3. Fear is particular because our personal experiences vary.

4. There are new threats that may cause us to develop new fears. Fear's power comes from our own thoughts and beliefs. So we allow fear to control us, when the truth is, we can control it. Without our acquiescence, fear has no power. When we rehearse our fears we lose focus on real problems. Worldly solutions fail (Romans 12:2).

5. The components of debilitating fear are:

Anxiety. Defined as: "an abnormal and overwhelming sense of apprehension of fear marked by such physical symptoms as tension, tremor, sweating, palpitation, and increased pulse rate." We all have moments of anxiety. Some verses that can help us overcome anxiety include: Proverbs 12:25 and Philippians 4:6-7.

Dread. Defined as: "an extreme fear-inspired reluctance to face or meet a particular person or situation." We all feel dread when we are forced to meet a judgmental authority figure (Exodus 15:15-16). A feeling of terror is often linked to dread.

Worry. Defined as: "mentally troubled or concerned . . . constrict, to press." Help is given in Luke 12:22-23 and 12:25-26. Concern is different from worry: this turns us to God to help us focus on our problems (Luke 12:31).

Phobia. Defined as: "an exaggerated and often disabling fear." A phobia is a fear of an object or situation that is disproportional to its actual danger.

Fright or panic. Defined as "terror excited by sudden danger." Fright is a short term intense fear. Panic occurs when we feel greater danger. It alerts our bodies to go into a self-protective mode with adrenalin pumping through us (Exodus 14:10-11).

Terrified. The most debilitating of all fears, imprisons us. Originates when we encounter extreme danger that could lead to our death. Our minds and bodies may freeze because we feel overcome with terror.

Steps to prevail overcome fear:

  1. Acknowledge that you are controlled by fear. Realize fear is controlling you. Fear tries to stay hidden and lives in denial and evasiveness. Need to face your fears and seek help.

  2. Pray to God about your fear. Bring your fear(s) to the Lord for strength, direction and His help to overcome them (Isaiah 41:10 and 1 Peter 5:7).

  3. Determine if lies are controlling you. Satan uses our fears by ensnaring us to believe his lies (John 8:44). Lies can cause us anxiety and panic. We must turn to Jesus for the truth; He will reveal any lie(s) (John 8:32).

  4. Read and memorize the Bible for direction. The Bible inspires us and gives us new direction to diminish fear (Psalm 119:105 and Isaiah 34:5). Psalms help us with our sort out our emotions. His Word brings us closer to Him.

  5. We seek His presence. When we connect with Jesus, at our time of fear, He brings us peace, even when facing death (Psalm 16:11). Relate with Jesus and we discover His presence brings joy and calm.

  6. Faith in God replaces fear. Our fear is exchanged for faith in Christ, and His principles (2 Timothy 1:7) tell us Satan loses his power when we no longer fear death. Then, we start trusting Christ completely and we are blessed with peace.

Debilitating fear is one of the strongest emotions that we feel. Because of its strength, we need Jesus to help us or we can slip into anger and subsequent bitterness. We need to remember to seek God's help and recall when Christ brought us safely through some danger. Then recollect the memory and we will defeat debilitating fear and save us from falling into bitterness.

Discussion Questions

1. Are you living in fear now? Which one?

2. What are the two origins of our fears? What is the real power behind our fear?

3. Name two components of fear?

4. Name the six steps to find deliverance from fear.

Chapter 7

Intentional Forgiveness Leading to Reconciliation

As we have seen from the six previous chapters, bitterness can infect our mind, spirit and heart in such a powerful way that our actions come under its control. The world normally copes with bitterness by using denial and/or being evasive. Denial is defined as: "refusal to accept or acknowledge the reality or validity of a thing or idea." By choosing denial, we either consciously or subconsciously refuse to accept the truth of our hurt. Denial is a form of self-protection that appears to work at first because we stop thinking about the painful situation. In reality, this action doesn't stop our emotions from churning up inside. Eventually, they will percolate to the surface causing strife and conflict. Consequently, we are fooling ourselves and keeping ourselves from dealing with the pain we've obviously experienced. We do this because of our latent fear of conflict, or of admitting that we have problems in our lives. We want life to run smoothly so we fail to recognize the messiness of how real relationships work. A biblical example of denial is Peter's denial of knowing Christ in Matthew 26:69-75: "... *a servant girl came to him. 'You also were with Jesus of Galilee,' she said. But he denied it before them all. 'I don't know what you are talking about,' he said.*

"Then he went out to the gateway, where another girl saw him and said to the people there, 'This fellow was with Jesus of Nazareth.'

"He denied it again, with an oath 'I don't know the man.'

"After a little while, those standing there went up to Peter and said, 'Surely you are one of them for your accent gives you away.'

"Then he began to call down curses on himself and he swore to them, 'I don't know the man!'

"Immediately a rooster crowed. Then Peter remembered the word Jesus had spoken: 'Before the rooster crows, you will disown me three

times.' And he went outside and wept." In these verses, we see Peter using three stages of denial. First, he tries to divert attention to something else. Next, he uses an oath to make his denial stronger. And lastly, he uses a curse. Oftentimes, we do the same thing when we are facing a difficult situation. We feel the pain of facing the truth, but we deny it when we are under pressure.

Evasiveness, on the other hand, is defined as "not direct, candid, or forthright . . . avoiding confrontation." Thus, evasiveness is when we purposely try to deceive the other person when we do know the truth. Avoidance of conflict rather than facing problems is such a destructive tactic that I will discuss it more thoroughly in Chapter 11 on conflict.

Another evasive tactic is to divert the conversation or attention to another more agreeable subject. In this way, the spotlight is shifted away from us to the other person, or to a neutral subject. Fear of confrontation underlies evasiveness. Both denial and evasiveness may seem to work temporarily, but they fail in the long-term because the issues don't disappear. Sometimes people even use a mixture of denial and evasiveness to muddle through their lives to avoid the hard discussions and difficult conflicts that may develop.

Courage is needed to face the conflict and possible rejection in our lives and relationships. The definition of courage is: "moral strength, perseverance to withstand fear or danger . . . resolute." The Bible calls on us to seek God for courage like King Hezekiah did when confronted by an army of 185,000 solders that had conquered several nations. This situation is narrated in 2 Chronicles 32:7-8 when Hezekiah says: *"Be strong and courageous. Do not be afraid or discouraged because the king of Assyria and the vast army with him, for there is a greater power that is with us than with him. With him is only the arm of flesh, but with us is the Lord our God to help us and fight our battles. And the people gained confidence from what Hezekiah the king of Judah said."* Then an angel of the Lord came and struck down the enemy's entire army in one night. We, too, need to follow this example by putting our faith in God to help us to face our issues and conflicts. He will give us the courage we need.

Because of the power of bitterness in our lives, a strong commitment is required to eliminate or reduce the sources of our bitterness. According to the Bible, a commitment to forgiveness is God's answer to remove the pain and destruction of bitterness in our lives. Forgiveness is defined as: "to cease to feel resentment against on account of a wrong committed." Sometimes, however, people seek "cheap forgiveness" by using a quick insincere apology to avoid the hard work of forgiveness and repentance. Lewis Smedes, the Christian psychologist, in his landmark book on forgiveness, *Forgive & Forget,* points this out: "Powerful and sneaky people use apologies as end runs around repentance ... They get by only because we have lost our sense of difference between repentance for wrong and apologies for bungling." That is why forgiveness needs to be intentional, which is defined as "having the mind or will concentrated on some end or purpose." To avoid "cheap forgiveness," I purposely decided that we all need to use the process of "intentional forgiveness" in our lives. Intentional forgiveness means that I resolve with all my heart and soul, with God's help, to take the steps to remove the bitterness from my life.

Gary Smalley and Ted Cunningham in their book, *From Anger to Bitterness,* state: "Forgiveness is the antidote to the bondage of destructive anger. In fact, the word forgiveness in Greek is actually two words put together: being released and being pardoned. When we release someone from an offense and pardon them we become freer ourselves." Forgiveness was used in New Testament times in reference to canceling a debt or releasing someone from the obligation of a contract, commitment, or promise. Thus, we see that forgiveness has three goals. First it releases (pardons) the offending person from our anger for hurting us. Secondly, it releases us from the burden of carrying around the weight of the hurt and anger in our hearts. Finally, forgiveness releases us from the potential sin of bitterness. It amazes me to realize that we can become sinners from an offense perpetrated on us, if we don't forgive the offender. As a result, we see that there is a greater price when we don't forgive. Earnie Larsen in his book, *From Anger to Forgiveness,* points out this high price of unforgiveness when he states:

"Forgiveness is the realization that the price we are paying for resentment is simply too high. The goal is to refuse to pay this price any longer. That is why we forgive."

God understands that allowing unresolved anger to become bitterness will destroy us physically, mentally and, most importantly, spiritually. Bitterness will result in us becoming controlled by Satan as he begins to reside in our hearts and minds and pulls us away from God's plan for us. We end up seeking revenge.

On the other hand, when we forgive, we give up the right to retaliate against the person who hurt us. Jesus affirms this when he calls on us to forgive others in Matthew 6:14: *"For if you forgive men when they sin against you, your heavenly Father will also forgive you. But, if you do not forgive men of their sins, your Father will not forgive your sins."* Jesus is telling us to remember how many sins He has forgiven us, so we will want to forgive others of their sins. In effect, we pass on the spirit of forgiveness to others so that they, too, can pass it on so that a spirit of forgiveness pervades everyone. According to Hebrews 12:15: *". . . bitterness can defile many"* while forgiveness can bless many. Lewis Smedes in his book, *Forgive & Forget*, speaks to this: "Forgiveness is God's invention for coming to terms with a world in which, despite their best intentions, people are unfair to each other and hurt each other deeply. He began by forgiving us. And he invites us all to forgive each other."

Forgiveness is demonstrating an essential form of love for others as shown in I Corinthians 13: 5-6: *"It (Love, parenthesis added) is not rude, it is not self-seeking, it is not easily angered, it keeps no record of wrongs. Love does not delight in evil, but rejoices with the truth. It always protects, always trusts, always hopes, always perseveres."* We know from our previous chapters that bitterness shows the opposite of these qualities. Additionally, Jesus says to go further and love our enemies, including those who have hurt us. In Luke 6:35-36 Jesus says: *"But love your enemies, do good to them and lend to them without expecting anything back. Then your reward will be great, and you will be sons of the Most High, because he is kind to the ungrateful and wicked. Be merciful, just as your Father in heaven is merciful."* While such an admonition seems hard, it points to Jesus' desire for us to love our enemies by forgiving their offenses against us. In this way no bitterness will creep into our hearts.

Janice and Pat were staff members at a Women's Teen Challenge. Both were saved and loved Jesus, yet both lived in constant strife with each other. It seemed as if they would unconsciously irritate each other whenever they talked. When one made a proposal, the other would often interpret the proposal as an attack on her. Both would also shoot verbal barbs at the other throughout the day.

Inside, both knew this situation was not what Christ wanted for them. Each developed a feeling of guilt and pain for her behavior, yet each felt powerless to change her actions. Janet, in frustration, called me to ask if I could meet with them to work out the problem. In fact, I met with the whole staff for five hours. During the course of our discussion, we discovered that Pat had been sexually abused as a child, and Janice had lived through the pain of her parents' divorce. These powerful events had left a wounded spirit in each woman. With tears, they each expressed how their woundedness had strongly affected their relationship with each other. We all felt their pain as they relayed their emotional stories. A feeling of empathy for each other also filled both women. Pat tearfully spoke to Janice, "I'm so sorry that I hurt you and caused you such pain. Please forgive me. I won't do that again." Janice responded by accepting Pat's apology and asking for her forgiveness of her actions. A spirit of relief and peace filled both women and the rest of us. We all thanked God.

Lewis Smedes in his book, *Forgive and Forget,* introduces the moral aspect of forgiveness when he quotes Scottish theologian H.R. MacIntosh: "Forgiveness is an active process of the mind and temper of a wronged person, by means of which he abolishes a moral hindrance to fellowship with the wrongdoer and reestablishes freedom and happiness of friendship." MacIntosh considers bitterness as a moral issue or sin because God states so in Ephesians 4:31: *"Get rid of all bitterness . . ."*

Paul in Galatians 6:7 also warns us: *"Do not be deceived; God cannot be mocked. A man reaps what he sows. The one who sows to please his sinful nature, from that nature will reap destruction."* One of the acts of the sinful nature is hatred, which in turn leads to bitterness. So if we sow hatred and revenge, we shall reap them back. Rick Renner in his Book, *Sparkling Gems from the Greek*, puts it clearly: "What you sow is exactly what you will reap. It is far better for you to sow mercy and forgiveness than to get into the business of sowing bitterness. Even though it may seem very difficult to forgive and let go of the offense, it is far easier to take this route than to sow wrong seed and thus get trapped in the destructive cycle of sowing and reaping bitterness and strife that will ultimately hurt your marriage and your children."

Other parts of forgiveness are:

1. Christians don't deny the pain of the offense, but choose to respond to Christ's higher calling.

2. Realize that you can't control the offender's choices.

3. Stop dwelling on the offense(s) and motive(s) of the other person and instead pray for their well-being.

4. Allow God to judge the offender in His own way and in His own time.

5. Drop any demand for repayment, if that is possible.

6. Don't repay the offender with cursing or verbal insults even though they insulted you.

7. Forgiveness is a commitment to God's command, not a feeling of when you are ready.

8. Walk in God's truth, not in the lies that the offender may have believed and acted on.

9. Adopt a Christ-like attitude of forgiveness when hurt by someone. Our first thoughts and actions are of forgiveness toward the offender. In effect, forgiveness takes control of our minds.

In summary, allow God instead of Satan to work in both of you, then God will heal the hurt in your heart. He will remove the spirit of revenge and give you a feeling of peace toward the offender. Simultaneously, He is convicting the offender's heart and applying consequences to him for his offense. He will do a far better job than you could ever do.

Forgiveness is not the following:

1. Quick and easy. It often will take time for God to work.

2. Allowing the offender to continue to abuse you. We need to leave and set a firm boundary with them.

3. Permitting myself or my children to be put in the care of the abuser again. With abuse, a trust has been broken and is not often forgotten.

4. Continuing to be close friends with the offender even though you have been hurt.

5. Acting as if nothing has happened between you and the offender.

6. Stopping expressing your anger in a respectful godly way.

7. Excusing or tolerating someone's bad behavior.

The above list shows some of the many misconceptions about forgiveness. After extending forgiveness, many people think that the relationship with the offender will return to the same basis as before the hurtful incident occurred. In fact, the closeness of the relationship depends upon how much **both** parties desire forgiveness. Often a trust has been broken, which will take time to repair. We can do our part and gain God's healing power, but we can't control the other person's free will.

Some barriers to granting full forgiveness:

1. Fear of rejection is a major obstacle because most people want to be liked by others.

2. Pride in our position so we think it is solely the responsibility of the other person to ask for forgiveness.

3. Allowing our emotions to takeover our actions so that we seek revenge.

4. Rationalizing the offender's action(s) so that they won't have to forgive.

5. Electing to allow the wound of the offender to control our thinking about it.

6. Only partially forgiving the offender for his/her actions.

7. Allowing the advice from friends or family vs. God to direct your forgiveness.

Fearing rejection and pride in our position are probably the strongest barriers to not granting forgiveness. When we do this, we demonstrate our lack of trust in Christ and His principles. Often when we are hurt, we allow emotions do take over our actions to our own detriment.

Summary:

1. The world's approach to dealing with bitterness:

a. Denial. Defined as: "a refusal to accept or acknowledge the reality or validity of a thing or idea . . ." A self-protective way to fool ourselves as it never works except for short periods.

b. Evasiveness. Defined as: "not direct, candid, or forthright . . . avoiding confrontation." You are trying to fool someone else when you know the truth.

2. Need for Forgiveness. Forgiveness is "to cease to feel resentment against an account of wrong committed." Need for forgiveness in the Bible (Matthew 6:14).

a. Cheap forgiveness. This is only an apology used to avoid the hard work of forgiveness and repentance.

b. Intentional forgiveness. This is having the mind or will concentrated on granting forgiveness.

c. Three goals of forgiveness. One, it releases (pardons) the offending person from our anger. Two, it releases us from the burden of carrying around the weight of the hurt and anger in our hearts. Finally, releases us from becoming bitter.

d. Bitterness, is a moral issue or sin. What H.R. MacIntosh considers bitterness a sin because it violates God's command (Ephesians 4:31).

e. Reaping what we sow. See Galatians 6:7.

3. Forgiveness includes:

a. Not denying the pain of the offense.

b. Realizing that you can't control the offender's choices.

c. Not dwelling on the offense, instead pray for the offender's well-being.

d. Allowing God to judge the offender.

e. Dropping any demand for repayment.

f. Refusing to repay the offender with cursing or verbal insults.

g. Using our will and not our emotion to forgive.

h. Walking in God's truth, not in the lies that the offender believed.

i. Adopting a Christ-like attitude of forgiveness. Allowing forgiveness to take control.

4. Forgiveness is not:

a. Quick and easy. It takes time for God to work.

b. Allowing the offender to continue to abuse you.

c. Allowing yourself or your children to be in the care of the abuser again.

d. Continuing to be close friends with the offender.

e. Acting as if nothing has happened between you and the offender.

f. Stopping to express anger in a godly way.

g. Excusing or tolerating someone's bad behavior.

5. Some barriers to granting full forgiveness:

a. Fear of rejection—a major obstacle.

b. Pride—other person is solely responsible for asking for forgiveness.

c. Allowing your emotions to take over and seeking revenge.

d. Rationalizing the offender's action—they don't have to forgive.

e. Allowing the offender's hurt to control your mind and spirit.

f. Only partially forgiving the offender for his/her actions.

g. Allowing the advice from friends or family vs. God to direct your forgiveness.

Discussion Questions

1. What is forgiveness? What does it mean to you to grant or receive forgiveness?

2. Name two of the nine parts included in forgiveness as listed above.

3. What are two of the things forgiveness is not?

Chapter 8
Steps for Forgiveness

We have seen the critical importance of forgiving others from the last chapter. To make forgiveness a normal functioning part of our lives, however, we need to go through each of the following steps:

Developing a firm Christ-like belief in our minds and souls. Such preparation is a critical initial step in developing a forgiving attitude in our lives. Remember, what we believe in our hearts determines what we think and, in turn, what we will do. As a result, it is necessary for us to strengthen our belief in Christ and his godly principles in our lives. Are we developing our spiritual walk daily with Bible reading, sincere prayer and worship? These **daily** spiritual exercises help create the fertile ground in which forgiveness can flourish and become an everyday part of our walk. Or, do we have an inconsistent walk with God, honoring Him only on Sundays and holy days?

People who have depended on God and His Word when going through the trials of life, have developed a mindset for forgiveness. Additionally, they fully realize that unforgiveness toward a brother/sister is a sin against God. So they know it is not an option to forgive, but a command. The Bible confirms this point in Matthew 6:15: *"If you do not forgive men their sins, your Father will not forgive your sins."* They fully understand that unforgiveness breaks our relationship with God, as well as with the offending person. They have been wounded by the injustice committed against them like everyone else but they have discovered the vital peace that forgiveness brings to their lives. In effect, through the power of the Holy Spirit, they have developed an attitude of thankfulness that enables them to extend forgiveness to others; yes, even to those who have hurt them.

Perhaps, you are now living in bitterness or resentment and don't have the spiritual mind discussed above. You may not even know Jesus as your Lord and Savior and forgiveness is the last thing on your mind. Thus, when you are hurt by someone, you use revenge to retaliate. Yet, you now see the futility of such responses and you don't want to live in it any longer. What do you do? Start by seeking God through prayer and reading the Gospel of John. That gospel will teach you about God's love for you. Gradually, you will find that you want to commune daily with God in prayer and Bible reading. You also may begin to see your need for fellowship with true believers in a Bible-believing church. Your mind will start to change. Romans 12:2 tells us there is a difference between worldly thinking and spiritual thinking: *"Do not conform any longer to the pattern of this world, but be transformed by the renewing of your mind."* Accordingly, a changed godly mind is vital to being able to break the cycle of hurt and revenge. The results are critical to gain peace in your life.

Develop an open heart where compassion reigns and the attitude of judgment decreases. While such a change may be difficult and take time, your perseverance with God's help will result in real change in your mind and heart. Increasingly, you will see how the Holy Spirit starts to change the soil in your mind to become more fertile with a forgiving attitude, as described in the first paragraph. Then your mind-set for forgiveness is now ready. Remember, the choice is yours.

Acknowledge your hurt. We need to recognize our pain but, at the same time, not let it control us. Many times, we try to minimize the pain by denying it as a way of avoiding the real issues. On the other hand, others exaggerate their pain out of proportion to what is really the truth. What is necessary for healing is for us to understand the truth behind our pain and its intensity. Seeking God's answers will yield us the real truth.

Seek to use intentional forgiveness with the offender. We become dedicated to the commitment to extend forgiveness, even if the offending party doesn't acknowledge it or even want it from us. Our human frailty often wants to avoid confrontation and difficult conversations. Consequently, there is a need to walk in the spirit of God and be intentional with our forgiveness because we are fighting our fleshly desires. We realize that we don't want to live in the world of bitterness because we now know of its grave dangers to us, and to our family and friends.

If you are now living in bitterness or resentment, it is critical to immediately confess this sin to the Lord and ask for His forgiveness. As Jim Wilson points out in his book, *How to be Free from Bitterness:* ". . . I have to see that it is evil, and that it is my sin and my sin only. I do not get rid of it through the other person saying he is sorry. I do not get rid of it if the other person quits or dies. I do not get rid of it any other way except calling it sin against the holy God, confessing it and receiving forgiveness." If you are the offender, such a confession is often best stated out loud to God as you express your personal remorse for what you did. If you are the victim, again expressing your forgiveness of the offender to God will free you of any bitterness. As a result, I am changing my focus from the pain of my hurt to God's plan for extending forgiveness and hopefully reconciliation. Remember it is for your mental and spiritual sake. To help you handle possible rejection, pray to God for the betterment of that person and yourself before any meeting with the offender.

If you are the victim, your forgiveness message needs to include the following:

Your forgiveness needs to be unconditional. Offended people sometimes will put conditions on their forgiveness because they just can't let go of all the pain they feel. They allow their pain to control their decision, which allows a vestige of bitterness to continue even if it is reduced. Gary Smalley and Ted Cunningham point out the need for unconditional forgiveness in their book, *From Anger to Intimacy:* "Many times we want to put conditions on our forgiveness. We say things like, 'I'll forgive you if you promise never to do this again' or 'When he shows remorse, then I'll know he is ready to be forgiven . . .' These statements fail to understand that forgiveness is far more than just a tool to restore relationships. It is also a tool to restore our own souls." Our focus needs to be on restoring our souls and helping the offender repair his soul. Later, we can work on reestablishing the relationship.

We need to understand that forgiveness does sometimes take time and is a process, given the gravity of some serious offenses. A feeling of hate often develops from some of the serious offenses and can be difficult to repair. Once the hate habit, however, takes residence in our hearts it will soon control our lives. I fully realize that abuse issues, as I discussed earlier in this book, need God's special intervention and time to be truly healed. My friend and Teen Challenge mentee, Junitio, hated his abuser and did not want to forgive him until Christ, through Theophastic Prayer, brought peace to his heart. Then, he was finally able to forgive his abuser and obtain true freedom from bitterness. Thus, I fully understand the important need for Christian therapists, when such serious issues are at the heart of the bitterness. For most situations, however, the offenses against us are not that deep, even though they hurt. The goal is to become completely free of **all** bitterness, which is why God calls for unconditional forgiveness.

Forgetting. Once you have forgiven the offender, you stop dwelling on any past offenses that the offender committed against you. You do not forget before you forgive them or there is nothing to forgive. Lewis Smedes highlights this timing in his book, *Forgive & Forget:* "Once we *have* forgiven, however, we get freedom to forget. This time forgetting is a sign of health; it is not a trick to avoid spiritual surgery. We can forget *because* we have been healed."

The goal of forgetting again is to achieve healing of the mind and spirit. The reason this is so important is if we are holding onto the pain of the offender's past offenses, we remain trapped in our bitterness. We remember that God forgives and forgets our sins. Consequently, we need to do the same to free ourselves.

Practice in private and with a close friend or relative. Practice your forgiveness message to yourself. Listen to your own words and how you say them. How you communicate your forgiveness is as important as the words themselves as stated in Proverbs 15:1:"*A gentle answer turns away wrath, but a harsh word stirs up anger.*" Ask a friend for feedback on your message and its delivery. Pray to God to help you communicate the words you need to say, not what you may feel like saying. Remember the admonition in Proverbs 12:18: "*Reckless words pierce like a sword, but the tongue of the wise brings healing.*" Now repeat what you want to say. Through the repetition, you will gain confidence in what you are planning to say.

Pray for the offender. Pray that God will remove any bitterness from both yourself and the offender. Also pray for the wrongdoer's health and care. Such prayers will soften your heart toward the offender and prepare you to have a Christ-like attitude when you "carefront" the offender. Paul Meyer in his book, *Forgiveness . . . the Ultimate Miracle,* states: "There is no way to hide unforgiveness at this level. If your forgiveness is genuine, you will know it . . . Prayer reveals what is in the heart." Watch out for the tendency to use prayer as a weapon against the offender, expecting God to impose His judgment on the wrongdoer. God will impose His judgment in His own way and time.

"Carefront" the person with your forgiveness message. This step is the hardest as you sense the emotional distance between you and the offender. This breach may lead him/her to rejecting your forgiveness message."Carefronting" means you show respect for the wrongdoer in your words and actions, when confronting them. You are heeding Christ's call to offer your forgiveness, despite the fear of rejection. Furthermore, it means that you are trying to do your best to respond kindly toward the offender, even when they have acted unkindly to you. As a sign of respect, keep your eyes focused on the other person's face. Remember that you are counting on God's help and He will convey your message of forgiveness to the offending person.

Speak in a respectful and humble way using "I" statements like "I was hurt when you said or did . . . but I want to forgive you completely from what you did." It is important to express the hurt the offender inflicted because sometimes they don't realize they have hurt you. At the same time, you are forgiving them so that the incident can be washed clean from your heart and mind. If the wrongdoer denies the incident or your forgiveness, don't press him. Let the Holy Spirit work on him/her. Realize that at least you have freed yourself from the poison of bitterness. If the offender accepts your forgiveness, praise God! Your action may spur him/her to repentance for what they did to you and may provide the impetus for reconciliation—the ultimate goal.

Continuing to pray for the offender. You pray for their well-being, even if they rejected your offer of forgiveness. While the Bible doesn't directly address this point, Jesus in Luke 6:27-28 tells us love and pray for our enemies: "*But I tell you who hear me: Love your enemies, do good to those who hate you, bless those who curse you, pray for those who mistreat you.*" Such prayers will continue to remove any residue of hatred or revenge in your heart and may bring God into the offender's life.

Dick had a neighbor who was very friendly when he first moved into the neighborhood. The neighbor seemed so curious about what Dick was doing to his house. Having two cars, Dick quickly realized that he needed to expand his one-car driveway toward the property line with his neighbor. He went to the town authorities and checked on all the proper procedures. Following their advice, he had a surveyor come and mark out his property line and he obtained a building permit. The neighbor was with Dick watching as the survey was being done and Dick told him of his expansion plans. The neighbor made no comment.

When the paving contractor started digging the new driveway, Dick's neighbor's face became contorted and he began screaming at Dick: "You can't put your driveway there!"

Dick didn't understand his neighbor's problem since it was all on Dick's own property. Basically, his neighbor wanted to have the edge of Dick's new driveway be at least one foot inward from the neighbor's property line. Dick had it at two inches away. The authorities had told Dick that he had permission to go up to the property line. Dick told him that he couldn't meet his request, as he wouldn't have sufficient room for his car. The neighbor immediately rushed to the authorities to stop Dick, but was unsuccessful. When the neighbor returned frustrated in his attempt, he angrily shouted "I'm not speaking to you again!" In effect, he was punishing Dick with his "silent treatment."

That Friday night, Dick went home somewhat dazed by the day's emotional events. He prayed to God for wisdom and continued to pray all weekend. God told him to go to his neighbor and forgive him and work out the conflict. Dick told Him he would do it despite the strong possibility of rejection. Later, Dick felt a true peace in his heart. Monday when Dick tried to talk and forgive his neighbor, his neighbor wouldn't listen and escorted Dick out of his house. His neighbor has not spoken to Dick or his wife now for over five years. Dick continues to pray for his neighbor. Dick is trusting God to work this out in His timing.

In this factual story, the different elements that lead to bitterness were present: differing expectations, harsh words spoken and the lack of acceptance of forgiveness. Disappointingly, Dick's neighbor elects to continue to live in a prison of bitterness with its painful effects on his life. Dick prays the neighbor will change.

THE EQUATION FOR FORGIVENESS

We had an equation showing the development for bitterness in chapter one. This new equation is designed to show you the path for forgiveness:

Holds a bitter spirit → convicted by God to forgive the offender → restores our connection with Christ → acknowledges the hurt → forgets past offenses → develops a forgiveness message → practices that message in private and with a friend or relative → prays for the offender → "carefronts" the person with a forgiveness message → continues to pray for the offender → receives God's peace → healing occurs → reconciliation possible.

As a Christian, God comes into our lives and convicts our hearts of the sin of bitterness. Sometimes God sends a messenger to do the convicting. In the Bible, God sent Nathan as His messenger to convict King David (2 Samuel 12:1-12) of his sin with Bathsheba. Once convicted, we want to forgive our offender, but first we must restore our spiritual connection with Christ that was severely weakened by our bitterness. We acknowledge our hurt and forgive the offender of his past transgressions against us. Next, we develop our forgiveness message and practice it in private and with a friend or relative to become confident with it. We pray for the offender to find healing and to receive our forgiveness. Then, we "carefront" the offender with our message using respectful words and actions. We continue to pray for the offender, whether he accepts or rejects our message. If we have been following God's direction and His principles of forgiveness, we shall receive a peace in our heart. Reconciliation is now possible between us and the offender.

The benefits of forgiveness:

1. Reclaiming a close relationship with God that is blocked when living in bitterness.

2. Feeling an inner sense of peace in one's life, as the weight of bitterness has been lifted.

3. The relationship with the offender is usually better. We may

never become close friends, although that has happened through forgiveness.

4. Developing a more compassionate heart toward those around us.

5. Creating relationships that are closer and more open, not as guarded as before.

Summary:
Steps for Forgiveness

a. Develop a firm Christ-like belief in our minds. Requires developing our spiritual walk with Bible reading, sincere prayer and worship. These actions create the fertile mind-set for forgiveness in our lives (Romans 12:2).

b. Acknowledge your hurt. Recognize our pain, but don't let it control us.

c. Seek intentional forgiveness. Commit to granting forgiveness even if the offending party doesn't acknowledge it or want it. Avoid the sin of unforgiveness.

d. Your forgiveness message. Needs to include the following:

1.) Forgiveness is unconditional. Offended people put conditions on their forgiveness because they can't let go of the pain.

2.) Forgetting. Refusing to meditate on any past offenses of the offender, otherwise we stay trapped in our bitterness.

e. Practice in private and with a close friend or relative. Practice it out loud to yourself. Listen to your words and how you say them. Ask a friend for feedback on your message (Proverbs 15:1 and 12:18).

f. Pray for the offender. Pray to remove all bitterness from you and the offender. Pray for the wrongdoer's health, which softens your heart toward the offender.

g. "Carefront" the person with your forgiveness message. "Carefronting" means showing care for the wrongdoer with respectful actions: keep your eyes focused on the other's face and use "I" statements in your forgiveness message. If the wrongdoer denies the offense or your forgiveness, don't press him/her.

h. Continue to pray for the offender. Pray for their well-being even if they rejected your forgiveness (Matthew 5:44).

Discussion Questions

1. Have you used any of the steps listed, when you granted forgiveness? What happened?

2. Were you able to forget the situation after you forgave the offender?

3. Were you able to pray for the offender? How did you feel afterward?

Chapter 9
Different Reactions to Forgiveness by Both Parties

Once we have declared our forgiveness message to the offender there are a number of different ways that the offender may respond. These include:

Denial of any wrongdoing. When the offender denies the wrong he/she has committed, in effect, they reject your overture to find resolution. Such a denial feels like the offender is intensifying his offense to what he has already done. Frequently, he/she may be holding onto their bitterness from some other event in their lives and are projecting their pain onto you. Erwin Lutzer addresses this type of denial in his book, *When You've Been Wronged: Moving from Bitterness to Forgiveness*: "Confront some people and they will resort to total denial; they are so incapable of seeing their sin that further discussion is a waste of time."

Basically the offender has become unreachable except by God. We need to remember not to allow the offender's bitterness to control our lives, but to pray for them and release our bitterness to God through prayer.

Blatantly rejecting your forgiveness. This response is when the offender discards your forgiveness message, as Dick's neighbor did to him. You felt called to follow Christ's admonition by granting forgiveness, so such a rejection feels like a shock. Such a reaction can cause you, if you are not fully intentional about forgiveness, to become even more angry at the offender and even embittered yourself. You may even feel angry at yourself for even extending forgiveness.

The offender may think that you have offended him/her in some real or imagined way, so they retaliate by hurting you. They become caught in their own bitterness and won't accept your forgiveness. As you recall from our first chapter, "hurt people hurt other people." There may have been a hurt in their upbringing, which leaves a lasting scar on their lives and they don't know how to receive forgiveness. Consequently, they bring their hurt into contact with you and respond to you out of their pain. In effect, they mistakenly want you to hurt like they were hurt. Unfortunately, this response is the normal worldly way. Such is the law of free will, which allows each person to decide for themselves. One would get the impression that we should not even try to forgive such difficult people. The Apostle Peter may have had similar thoughts, Matthew 18:21-22 states: "*Then Peter came to Jesus and asked, 'Lord how many times shall I forgive my brother when he sins against me? Up to seven times?' Jesus answered, 'I tell you, not seven times, but seventy-seven times.'*" This leads us into our next section.

One-sided forgiveness. Despite your hurt feelings from the offender's rejection(s) mentioned above, you still realize that you are still convicted to follow Christ's command to grant forgiveness and maintain an attitude of grace in your heart toward the offender. With the Holy Spirit's help, you don't allow the offender's rejection to control your thoughts and attitude toward them. This attitude reflects your desire to be intentional in your forgiveness despite their negative response. Such resolve frees you from the bondage of potential bitterness and puts you in a position to receive God's peace as described in Philippians 4:7: "*And the peace of God, which transcends all understanding, will guard your hearts and minds in Christ Jesus.*" This peace, from the strife of bitterness, is such a blessing in our lives. Erwin Lutzer, describes one-sided forgiveness further in his book: "Yes, I believe in what I call one-sided forgiveness. Bitterness must be released from our lives, or we are the losers. If you have been offended, you need to forgive the one who has wronged you. When we don't forgive those who have wronged us, our lives remain under the control of those who have done us the most damage. Let me say it again: Don't let their sin ruin your life." It is interesting that we think that we are in control by not forgiving, but the reality is our bitter attitude is the one in control.

Randy and Sam had been best friends since their youngest years in a small town in upstate NY. They bonded together, starting in their teens, through similar interests. Later they shared a love for riding motorcycles. As they grew up, they separated geographically, but they still got together to ride their bikes and explore the countryside. This close true friendship stayed alive through their thirties and into their fifties.

One day, however, Sam was killed instantly in an accident while he was riding his motorcycle by a lady who had been drinking and driving. Randy felt crushed as his best friend was lowered into the ground. He felt such hatred towards the woman who had done this. She refused, however, to take responsibility and fought the charges in court with a high-priced team of lawyers. Randy attended the trial, and his anger grew as he witnessed the woman's attempts to deny her guilt.

Realizing that his anger was turning into bitterness, Randy, who was a Christian, started researching forgiveness in the Bible. He also started praying for the woman and gradually his hatred left him. Finally, he felt compelled to grant her his forgiveness, but when he tried to forgive her, she wouldn't accept his forgiveness message. Despite this disappointing rejection, he realized that his heart was completely free of its former bitterness. She was sentenced to three to five years in jail, but only served two years for good behavior. Randy is leaving the final judgment to God.

You too, may have a lingering desire to have your forgiveness acknowledged by the offender and achieve mutual forgiveness (two-sided) forgiveness. Some people mistakenly expect that if they sincerely forgive someone, everything will be friendly between both parties. Consequently, they have an emotional letdown when the other person fails to respond with remorse, or replies negatively. In such a case we need to remember that we have taken the Christ-like action. Moreover, we will still receive the peace of God from our bitterness as discussed above. We need to remember that it takes the **desire** in **both** parties to achieve the next stage—two-sided forgiveness.

Two-sided forgiveness. This type occurs when the victim forgives the offender, as set forth above, and the offender acknowledges the forgiveness. Below are the steps the wrongdoer needs to follow in order to restore the relationship:

> **Acknowledge the hurt that you inflicted.** Pain brings out our emotions, especially in the victim that was hurt. The offender realizes what he has done and takes responsibility for causing the hurt. Such a positive action starts to show the offender's empathy for the victim.

> **Express remorse for what you did.** Remorse is more than sorrow. It is defined as: "gnawing distress arising from a sense of guilt for past wrongs." Many wrongdoers are sorry that they got caught. At such times, offenders often express quick apologies like, "I'm sorry that I ..." usually with little emotion. Such pat expressions provide little help as they only serve to antagonize the victim.
>
> The wrongdoer needs to truly feel and express deep sorrow with emotion. This demonstrates that there has been a real change in their heart and attitude. A powerful biblical example of honest remorse is David confessing to God in Psalm 51:3: *"For I know my transgressions and my sin is always before me."* When someone expresses similar remorse, you sense the authenticity of their sorrow for the injury they com-

mitted. Their hearts have been transformed toward mending the relationship. Lewis Smedes reinforces this point in his book, *Forgive and Forget:* "When you tell those you hurt that you realize what you did was intolerable and that you share their pain, you reach the level of confession. If they believe you, your separate sadnesses will melt into one."

Humbly ask for forgiveness. When the offender has developed the vital groundwork of the above steps, then the wounded person is looking for such a forgiveness request. It is vital for the offender to express humbleness, not a demand, when asking for forgiveness. Such humbleness reflects sincerity as shown in Proverbs 3:34: *"He mocks proud mockers but gives grace to the humble."*

Offer restitution where applicable. Restitution is paying back what was taken or damaged. Such action reflects a sincere desire to restore the financial or physical damage the offender did. This option is not possible when careless or harmful words caused the wound. In the Bible, Zacchaeus, the tax collector, demonstrates restitution beyond what is expected in Luke 19:8: *"... if I have cheated anyone out of anything, I will repay him back four times the amount."* Zacchaeus was exceeding the command requiring restitution for stealing, as set forth in Leviticus 6:5: *"... He must make restitution in full, add a fifth of the value to it...."*

Be repentant. Means "to turn from sin out of penitence for past wrongdoings." Such contrition reflects the offender's verbal commitment to not commit the same offensive act again, for the sake of the relationship. The acid test will be if their future behavior matches their verbal commitment and they don't revert back to their old hurtful words or action(s).

Limited Forgiveness. In some cases, forgiveness is sincerely extended by an offended person to free himself of bitterness but, for good reasons, he limits his trust of the offender. Such painful situations include: abuse situations, hurting his child or spouse, adultery, stealing valuable property, etc. In these illustrations there is a demonstrable lack of trust. As a result of these serious offenses, he/she forgives the person, but does not trust them immediately, or sometimes ever again. Trust, in these situations, is only earned from corrected behavior over time to insure that the offender has truly repented. Other times, as in sexual abuse offenses, trust may never be extended. It is important to the victim's spiritual health to still release his/her anger through forgiveness. Erwin Lutzer, in his book, *When You've Been Wronged: Moving from Bitterness to Forgiveness*, points out the effect of an offender giving superficial forgiveness: "... he does not understand the depth of the pain and hurt that he caused. If we trivialize what the other party considers serious, there cannot be full reconciliation. Keep in mind that *when sin is viewed superficially, it is dealt with superficially.*" Thus asking for, and giving forgiveness, is serious because offended people feel wounded. The offender needs to clearly demonstrate sincere repentance in words and long-term change, if true two-sided forgiveness is to be achieved.

> Donald had been raised in a rural family. His father would explode with anger and violence if Donald did something wrong. As a result, Donald would stay quiet and try his best to avoid his father. The irony was that he still looked up to his father. One day his father showed him a new golf club that he had purchased. He told Donald, "Just hit a few balls in the back field." Donald was very excited since he had never hit a golf ball. So he happily proceeded to hit the balls, which progressively went further and further. Finally, on the last ball, he blasted it and the ball took off and crashed through the windshield of his father's van parked at the far end of the yard. Donald immediately ran into the house trying to hide from his father's wrath.

His father, upon hearing the crash, ran outside shouting for Donald. The father searched for Donald and found him huddled in fear in his closet. Donald pleaded with his father, "Please dad don't beat me," but to no avail: his father proceeded to both kick and beat him mercilessly. The beating went on and on despite Donald's pleas to stop. When it was over, Donald's face was so badly beaten his parents kept him from going to school for three days. They were concerned that the authorities might become suspicious of his wounds.

This beating was one of many Donald received from his father until he got too big for his father and the beatings stopped. Later, Donald drifted into drugs which medicated the pain he felt from his father's thrashings. Donald came into Syracuse Teen Challenge and asked me for a healing of this memory. Using Theophastic Prayer, Christ brought Donald peace from this painful memory. He limits his involvement with his father, however, because his father still tries to exert his old control but he has forgiven his father for those agonizing beatings.

The benefit of two-sided forgiveness is that the relationship, if any, can start to be restored. If you have hurt someone, don't expect full restoration from the victim if he/she feels they were hurt deeply. Trust needs to be built up with time. Full reconciliation takes time as discussed in the next chapter.

Summary:
Different reactions by the offender to forgiveness:

1. No acknowledgement or rejection of forgiveness. Offender denies the wrong he/she committed and rejects the offender's forgiveness. They want us to hurt like they do. Unless we forgive, this reaction can cause us to become bitter again.

2. One-sided forgiveness. You are convicted by the Holy Spirit to still grant forgiveness to the offender.

3. Two-sided forgiveness. Parties forgive each other. The offender needs to:

> **1.) Accept responsibility for the hurt.** Starts the empathy process.

> **2.) Express remorse for what they did.** Remorse is "gnawing distress arising from a sense of guilt for past wrongs" (Psalm 51:3).

> **3.) Humbly ask for forgiveness.** Vital to express humbleness when asking for forgiveness (Proverbs 3:34).

> **4.) Offer restitution where applicable.** Paying back what was taken or damaged (Luke 19:8 and Leviticus 6:5).

> **5.) Be repentant.** Turn from sin out of penitence for past wrongs. Does the offender stop hurting you in the same way?

4. Limited Forgiveness. Forgiveness is extended. The hurt party limits their trust of the offender because of: abuse, adultery, stealing, etc. Trust must be earned over time.

Discussion Questions

1. Have you used one-sided forgiveness? What happened?

2. Have you experienced two-sided forgiveness?

3. Have you had to use limited forgiveness?

4. What feelings did you experience when you granted forgiveness?

Chapter 10
Reconciliation with the Offender

One of our major goals in life should be to try to repair damaged relationship(s) through reconciliation with an offender, especially if they are a family member or close friend. The emotional damage from unresolved conflict causes us deep anguish as well as negatively affects those with whom we are in conflict. The former close intimacy has been fractured, if not irrevocably broken, and at this point an emotional distance has developed.

Assuming both parties have achieved the steps for two-sided forgiveness as set forth in the last chapter, there is an opportunity, with God's help, for complete reconciliation of the relationship. Reconciliation means "to restore to friendship, compatibility or harmony." Jesus calls us in Mathew 5:24 to: *". . . be reconciled with your brother."* Thus, reconciliation is a command from Christ that we should strongly desire to accomplish with His help. Having successfully achieved the steps for full forgiveness, usually there is a mutual desire to regain the former relationship. We want to again feel that special connection with that person again. However, our trust of each other has been damaged, if not destroyed. The steps for achieving full reconciliation for each party are as follows:

A Commitment from both parties for reconciliation. Ideally, each party feels that the relationship is so vital that they both will make its restoration a priority. Such a commitment means that each party is willing to make corrections to their own behavior. Each seeks to find out what they did wrong and how they can correct their own words and actions.

Praying to God. Bringing God into this process is critical as He will guide both parties with what actions to take and what to say to each other. First, both parties must reconcile with God by confessing their sinful actions and ask for His forgiveness and for reconciliation with the other person. Such a humbling act draws God closer to both of them. Then, He can bless both parties through the ministry of reconciliation. As stated in 2 Corinthians 5:18: *"And this is from God, who reconciled us to himself through Christ and gave us the ministry of reconciliation . . . ."* Note if only one party does this step, the process reverts back to one-sided forgiveness.

Listening to the other party to understand them. James 1:19 states: *"Be quick to listen slow to speak and slow to become angry."* Listen not only to the words but also the emotions expressed. Listening is not necessarily agreeing, but shows great respect for the other person. When both parties intently listen to understand the other person's pain, this is a powerful step toward reconciliation.

Expressing your hurt and a desire to forgive each other. Sometimes each party feels that the other person has offended them. Expressions of their hurt, together with mutual forgiveness, presented in a humble, god-like manner draws both parties back together.

Seeking forgiveness with persistence. Sometimes only one party wants reconciliation but through that party's persistence, restoration of the relationship is eventually achieved. If you are the persistent person, take the initiative by being the first to forgive. Also, express your commitment to the relationship and request that you both meet regularly to rebuild trust. Realize that over time the other person will test your commitment to restoration. Don't give up unless the other person completely resists you numerous times.

In Teen Challenge I have seen this reconciliation process work successfully with men who were divorced from their wives. It requires God working in both parties, and the men being persistent and honest with their wives. After this hard work, these men remarried their ex-wives and had a much stronger relationship. The true-life story below demonstrates the power of reconciliation in two lives that were shattered by bitterness.

> Marlene had seen Jane in church over several years, but she had never really talked with her. Marlene was 15 years older, so she thought that there would be no possible chance of connecting. Then, at a church gathering, Jane approached Marlene for the first time and started talking to her. She said she wanted to be friends and soon they were sharing the personal details of their lives. They agreed to meet the next week for lunch. The meeting went very well as they discovered they had many similar interests. Their connection continued to grow closer over the weeks of meetings and soon they became best friends.
>
> After several years, however, one day Jane heard from someone else that Marlene had not defended her from some malicious gossip. Jane felt betrayed and erupted in anger at Marlene: " Why didn't you defend me when you heard that gossip about me? Why didn't you stop that gossip?" Marlene felt shocked at the extent of Jane's resentment. She initially tried to justify her actions, but finally apologized sincerely for not defending her. She also promised to defend Jane in the future from such malicious comments. Furthermore, she committed to meeting with her more regularly and prove her loyalty over time. Thus, Marlene used the steps of reconciliation and the relationship was restored and became even stronger.

This story demonstrates how relationships will encounter times of severe disagreement. How that clash is handled by the parties can easily determine the future of that relationship.

The benefits of reconciliation are enumerated below. Some of the concepts come from Erwin Lutzer's book: *When You've Been Wronged: Moving from Bitterness to Forgiveness:*

> **Our attempts at reconciliation are a witness to the world.** Look at Christians when they have conflict and division to see if they are able to reconcile their issues or act in the same way as the world. Effectively, whether we like it or not, we are role models to unbelievers who may be seeking new constructive ways of resolution. Also, they are watching to see if we will follow our Christian principles such as: "loving our neighbors as ourselves."
>
> **We pursue reconciliation to influence our future generations.** Having seen or experienced the pain of bitterness and its isolation, we must have a goal of preventing it from spreading to future generations. As I mentioned earlier, I am a product of such a division in my own family. I can still remember the grief of separation from my cousin over a minor issue that wasn't resolved between my mother and her sister.
>
> **We see disunity in the body of Christ without reconciliation.** Often there are divisions and splits in the church when we allow Satan to control our actions in regards to minor issues, instead of pursuing forgiveness and reconciliation. Believers, who get caught up in such worldly actions, often lose their desire for church and other Christian activities.
>
> **We Christians demonstrate the power of the gospel.** The power of reconciliation in Christians' lives shows God's healing power in conflicts to unbelievers. When this happens, unbelievers are drawn to the gospel and its message.
>
> **Reconciliation restores close relationships that are vital to our lives.** We all encounter conflict in our relationships, which may result in dividing us. Reconciliation not only brings us back together, but many times increases our feelings of closeness to the other person. Such deeper intimacy is a benefit that God gives us

from doing the hard work of true reconciliation.

Reconciliation brings peace into our lives again. From the strife of conflict, we want to find tranquility again in our lives. True reconciliation will bring that as long as we follow the above steps. We all desire to see the power of reconciliation in our lives to overcome the anguish of broken relationships. I hope that this chapter has given you hope to repair your broken relationships that are now controlled by bitterness.

Summary:

Reconciliation. Defined as "to restore to friendship, compatibility or harmony" (Mathew 5:24)

Steps for achieving reconciliation for each party are:

1. A Commitment from both parties. Each is willing to forgive and correct their own behavior to restore the relationship.

2. Praying to God. He will guide both parties' actions. We must reconcile with God by confessing our sins and asking for forgiveness.

3. Listening to understand each other. Both parties are intent to listen to understand the other person.

4. Expressing their hurt and forgive each other. Both parties express their hurt, together with humble forgiveness to draw the parties together.

5. Seeking forgiveness with persistence. When one party persists in forgiveness, such persistence often leads to reconciliation. Keep trying to meet regularly to rebuild mutual trust.

The advantages of reconciliation are:

1. Our attempts at reconciliation is a witness to the world. As

Christians, we are role models in our behavior toward each other and the world.

2. We pursue reconciliation to influence our future generations. We develop a goal of preventing bitterness from spreading to future generations.

3. We see disunity in the body of Christ without reconciliation. Disunity is a sign that Satan has gained control in our churches and families. Believers caught up in such conflicts often lose their desire for church.

4. We Christians demonstrate the power of the gospel. Reconciliation in Christians' lives shows God's healing power in conflicts, causing unbelievers to be drawn to the gospel.

5. Reconciliation restores close relationships that are vital to our lives. Reconciliation not only restores the relationship, but God blesses us with increased intimacy for the other person.

6. Reconciliation brings peace into our lives again. Instead of the strife of conflict, we find tranquility in our lives.

Discussion Questions

1. What is reconciliation?

2. Have you ever used any of these steps when trying to reconcile? Did they work?

3. Do you find that learning these steps gives you the confidence to try reconciliation in the future?

4. Do you feel the benefits of reconciliation make it worth trying?

Chapter 11
Conflict Patterns:
Escalation and Avoidance

Most of us are unaware of how easily we can get caught in a deadly pattern of conflict with someone close to us. Such patterns can easily spiral us into bitterness. Our story of Will and Joe in Chapters 4 and 5 reflect this situation. Conflict is defined as "a clash, competition, or mutual interference of opposing forces of ideas or interests." It arises out of differences between people such as: age, gender, race, values, ideas, etc. No one can avoid conflict as we all experience it many times in our lives. Like anger, conflict allows us to have a choice as to how we express ourselves and act. Unlike anger, conflict requires at least two people to be involved: they are clashing over something. We don't have conflicts with dogs, our car, or a stove, but we may express anger at them.

When we are involved in an interpersonal clash, anger is often expressed in a negative way. As a result of the negativity, such arguments become painful to one, or both participants. Dr. Les Carter discusses how conflict becomes negative in his book, *The Anger Trap*: "When conflict and aggravation arise, anger is expressed because of a desire for closure . . . Problems arise, however, when the need for closure is so strong that individuals convince themselves they cannot find peace until they succeed in ordering their world to be precisely as they wish." To win a disagreement on our own terms, we frequently employ a familiar conflict pattern in expressing our views and wants to someone. A pattern in this instance is defined as: "a reliable sample of traits, acts or other observable features characterizing an individual." In effect, conflict patterns become our frequent means of expression in arguments. We may consistently use one pattern with all arguments. On the other hand, some people may use one pattern for offense and an entirely different one for defense in their disagreements to either gain advantage or avoid pain. The problem is that there are both positive and negative patterns. The negative patterns, while comfortable to use, don't resolve the conflicts. Instead, they create frustration often leading to bitterness.

We develop these patterns, either positive or negative, in early childhood when we observe the verbal and nonverbal ways of our parents' conflict. By repeatedly witnessing our parents' approaches to conflict, we internalize or "imprint" their pattern of conflict expression into our minds. Milan & Kay Yerkovich in their book, *How We Love*, discuss how this imprint is mainly connected with how we love; it also applies to how we deal with conflict. "Our experiences growing up, good and bad, left a lasting imprint on our souls that determined our beliefs and expectations . . . ." Later they state: "Most of us had hurtful experiences resulting in a harmful imprint . . . ." Consequently, we develop our own pattern of conflict from watching our parents' conflicts. Because of these youthful imprints, we frequently copy our parents' negative pattern of expressing conflict without realizing it. Ironically, these patterns aren't effective, but they feel so familiar to us that we often use them anyway.

Factors that help determine the type of conflict patterns we use are as follows:

Our close relationship to one parent. Because we want to be like them, we choose their type of conflict pattern, which reflects the positive imprint we received from that parent. Unfortunately, that parent's conflict expression may not be positive.

We have a difficult parental relationship. Here the imprint is so strong, even if we disliked the conflict pattern, we often end up adopting it ourselves. This approach often becomes a generational curse that continues through succeeding generations.

Our personalities. Aggressive personalities are drawn to use the critical pattern of conflict while a passive child will be drawn to the avoider, or vacillator model.

> When I was young, I remember being shy and not aggressive. Consequently, my father's shouting and aggressive form of conflict seemed very fearful to me. My response was simply to escape from his fearful shouting. The result was I became an avoider of conflict as best as I could. Later, after I got married and a conflict developed with my wife, I would feel a powerful urge to leave the room immediately. I could actually feel my feet wanting to walk out of the room while I was still sitting. In other words, I had a strong imprint to avoid conflict whenever it arose. Yet at my workplace, I soon realized I could no longer withdraw like that. Now I had to stay in the conflict and express myself in more positive assertive ways. Later, after reading books about conflict, I learned there are positive ways to express anger that achieve better results.

The conflict pattern that seems to win the conflict. It is natural to want to win our own conflicts. If we see that shouting and harsh words win, we are inclined to use that approach ourselves for self-centered reasons.

The following four different negative conflict patterns were first developed in late 1980s at The University of Denver under a program called PREP (Prevention and Relationship Enhancement Program). The program was developed from research studying 135 married couples for 12 years. The results were first published in 1994 in their landmark book, *"Fighting for Your Marriage,"* by Howard Markman, Scott Stanley and Susan Blumberg. This study proved that these negative conflict expressions were devastating to 91% of the marriages. These factors were further expanded upon by Scott Stanley in his book, *A Lasting Promise: A Christian Guide to Fighting for your Marriage.* "People using these types of expression before marriage thus face difficulties or divorce in the marriage." The study demonstrated that it is critically important to change from these negative patterns to the positive one, set forth later in Chapter14. In reality, what is true for marriage is also true for any relationship. The following describes two of the four negative conflict patterns:

Escalation or criticism. When we use this type we are trying to win the clash on our terms through shouting, swearing, being judgmental and other forms of intimidation. This controlling method may actually work for us for a while, particularly with someone afraid of conflict. When using this pattern, we frequently feel an appealing sense of power and control. Consequently, we continue to use this method until we are stopped by someone, or we get convicted by God. This type is popular with men and those with aggressive personalities.

There is often a strong element of pride involved in this pattern and the combatant may act in a superior "know it all" way. In reality, many times critics have weak self-esteem and their posturing is only a way to avoid looking at their own weaknesses. This lack of humility often prevents them from receiving help for their own problems. Many of the persons using escalation, often use denial to handle their issues. They tend to be direct and uncompassionate in their interactions. They can force you to see your problems, but their distasteful presentation turns people away from listening to them. Tim Ursiny discusses the aspects of the critical person in his book, *The Coward's Guide to Conflict:* "Sometimes people act as though they are superior because they actually think they are better than others. Sometimes they act superior because their self-esteem is extremely low and they are trying to prove themselves. On other occasions, people shift to the critical mode as a defense because it feels safer than feeling hurt."

Frequently, people using escalation will use threats to enforce their ideas and values onto someone opposing them. Usual threats may include: leaving a marriage or relationship, firing you from a job, not giving love or intimacy, or not talking to you. In trying to win the argument, they will stretch the truth and exaggerate their side of the argument. Also, they will withhold information helpful to the other side. They do not really listen or try to understand the other person's viewpoints, so the receiver feels put down and, therefore, usually rejects what the critical person is espousing.

In marriages, escalation starts with small irritating events that start a conflict like, "You're so lazy that you can't even pick up your own clothes." Or, "You make too much noise when you eat." These small irritations get escalated into major battles when one spouse attacks the other in harsh aggressive ways. The receiving spouse often responds in self-protection using the same aggressive pattern. Howard Markman, Scott Stanley and Susan Blumberg point this out in their book, *Fighting for Your Marriage:* "One of the most damaging things about arguments that are escalating out of control is that people say things that threaten the very life-blood of their marriage, things that are not easily taken back." The harsh words in the escalation become hurtful as if one is driving a knife into the other's heart. As described in Proverbs 12:18: *"Reckless words pierce like a sword."* When one spouse receives such wounds, trust in the other starts to diminish and soon the spouse becomes cautious and less revealing. An atmosphere of insecurity starts to prevail between the spouses. Now the once openness of their close relationship starts to disappear as each member starts to protect his/her own feelings. Soon each spouse becomes more guarded in revealing his/her real feelings and emotions and the relationship could be on the way to destruction.

Below we see a real life example of escalation:

When I was working in the Real Estate Department of a bank, an important customer confronted me using escalation. He was very intent on getting more loan proceeds from me for the many modifications he had made to his real estate project. The problem was that all the changes were not increasing the loan value of the project, which prevented me from lending him more funds. Only more leasing, according to lending criteria, would allow me to extend him more funds.

Initially, he spoke in his normal voice requesting the

funds needed to cover these additional costs. I responded calmly that "I am unable to extend more funds to you" but I also suggested a possible solution. Instead of accepting my idea, however, he lashed out harshly, "I need those additional funds now! I'm not accepting your proposition." His voice started rising and profanities spewed forth. He screamed at me, "Get me those . . . funds now or I'll get your . . . job! I'll also take your house away."

This intimidation tactic was what he usually did when he could not get his way. All the other people in the room, mostly his people, were now staring at both of us wondering what would happen next. The fact that he was my most valuable client, I could feel the intense pressure to concede to his strong coercion. Being a Christian, I prayed internally to God. I felt Him telling me to hold my position and not to give in. I had tried by being respectful to avoid this conflict. Finally, I told him calmly, but firmly, that I still could not lend him the funds but I would review the situation with my boss. As I continued to talk calmly and with confidence from God, his volume diminished and there were with no more swear words. Later, my boss told me that, if I had submitted to the client's demands, I could have been fired. Praise God for His direction!

In this example, we see the various characteristics of the critical type of conflict: intimidation, loud voice, harsh words and an air of superiority. Imagine if I had responded with the same type of voice and language. Yet, that is what many people do as they get caught in the same critical trap as the offender. The key is to not respond in kind to such a tactic but express an opposite godly spirit.

In 2 Samuel 16:5-13, David has to contend with an escalation conflict and he shows us how to properly handle it: *"As King David approached Bahurim, a man from the same clan as Saul's family came out from there. His name was Shimei son of Gera, and he cursed as he came out. He pelted David and all the king's officials with stones, though all the*

*troops and the special guard were on David's right and left. As he cursed,
Shimei said, 'Get out, get out, you man of blood, you scoundrel! The Lord
has repaid you for all the blood you shed in the household of Saul, in whose
place you have reigned. The Lord has handed the kingdom over to your
son Absalom. You have come to ruin because you are a man of blood!'*

"Then Abishai son of Zeruiah said to the king, 'Why should this dead
dog curse my lord the king? Let me go over and cut off his head.'

"But the king said, 'What do you and I have in common, you sons of
Zeruiah? If he is cursing because the Lord said to him, 'Curse David,' who
can ask, 'Why do you do this?'

David then goes on: *"'My son, who is of my own flesh, is trying to
take my own life. How much more, then, this Benjamite! Leave him alone;
let him curse, for the Lord has told him to. It may be that the Lord will see
my distress and repay me with good for the cursing I am receiving today.'*

"So David and his men continued along the road while Shimei was
going along the hillside opposite him, cursing as he went and throwing
stones at him and showering him with dirt." Here David showed great
patience, despite the abuse he received. He maintained his composure
when confronted with unjustified criticism. David was not responsible
for Saul's death. What we have to remember is that the Lord will vindi-
cate us in the long run when we don't resort to escalation. The important
point to remember is that this critical pattern leads to negative results.

Escalation can also be shown in subtle ways like rolling of one's eyes,
throwing up hands in exasperation, muttering to oneself, etc. While
less dramatic, these nonverbal actions speak negatively to the other
person and often reflect what a person really feels. Words and nonverbal actions need to work together to present a consistent message. Men
tend to be less verbal and may tend to employ these nonverbal tactics.

Kerby Anderson, in his article, *Why Marriages Fail*, states: "Research shows that couples who have a good marriage are less prone to
escalation. And if the argument starts to escalate, they are able to stop
the negative process before it erupts into a full-blown fight." Kerby goes
on: "Couples who want a strong marriage must learn to counteract the
tendency to escalate as a couple . . . The key is . . . learning to control

your emotions and learning how to keep a rein on your tongue."

Another way to change from using escalation is to develop more patience in expressing your frustrations and anger. Respect is lacking in the escalation expression and results in failure and frustration leading to bitterness. Consequently, if we find ourselves using this approach, we need to recognize it and change it to the positive approach discussed in Chapter 14.

Withdrawal or Avoidance. This approach is motivated by a fear of conflict. The person dislikes the messiness of conflict with its angry voices and difficult tensions. Often times the person's personality is also more quiet and subdued. They do not feel safe emotionally to remain in the conflict, so they remove themselves emotionally and physically. Their sense of anxiety may cause them to get up and actually leave the room while someone is talking to them. They struggle with making their own needs known. Therefore, they develop an internal unexpressed anger at the other person and even themselves for lacking the courage to express their needs. Such anger often comes out in passive-aggressive ways like: being late, purposely doing a bad job, and purposely refusing to do something that you want them to do. The person using avoidance acts and speaks in the exact opposite way from the critical/ escalator who is so forthright, loud and aggressive. The withdrawer will sometimes withdraw permanently from the relationship and feel justified in so doing. They have such a strong yearning to avoid talking about difficult issues that they may never address them. They use denial of the problem as a defense mechanism. Basically, they are letting their fear of conflict and facing their problems control their actions. As a result, they may never resolve a conflict, or do so only with great difficulty. The irony is that sometimes an avoider will marry a critic so that chaos reigns in the relationship until someone changes.

It is important to realize that there may be circumstances in a conflict that may require a "time-out" when one, or both of the participants, are too emotional to listen to each other. Such a break allows the emotion to dissipate so that true dialogue—listening then talking without interrupting—can continue. During the time-out, I strongly recommend using that time to pray to God to calm down the emotions. Be aware that it may require several time-outs until the emotion of the participant(s) is diminished; perseverance is required. From my personal experience, this helpful concept will be successful, but it requires patience. Remember, the other person may not want to pray with you and may even keep talking to you while you are praying. Just don't give up, God will help you.

David in 2 Samuel 13 demonstrates this negative style of avoidance in his relationship with his children. First, his daughter Tamar is raped by her half brother, Amnon. In 2 Samuel 13:21 it states: "*When King David heard all this he was furious.*" Yet David avoided disciplining Amnon. This lack of handing out consequences leads another son, Absalom, to hold hatred for Amnon and to eventually seek revenge. The following verse reveals Absalom's heart condition: "*Absalom never said a word to Amnon, either good or bad; he hated Amnon because he had disgraced his sister Tamar.*" Two years later, we see how revenge can occur and how bitterness can remain for a long time. Absalom entices Amnon to a special meeting of all of King David's sons. Absalom gets Amnon drunk and tells his men in verse 13:28: "'*Strike Amnon down, then kill him.*'" This Absalom's men did, and he fled to his grandfather in fear of David's retaliation, which never came. In verse 13:39: "*And the spirit of the king longed to go to Absalom . . .*" However, again, David avoids doing anything until he is cajoled into inviting Absalom back to Jerusalem. Even then he misses an opportunity for restoration with his eldest son. Instead David decides in verse 13: 24: "*He must go to his own house; he must not see my face.*"

Later Absalom, in his anger at David, leads a rebellion that ends in his own death. David and his family experienced deep pain and anguish because he avoided handling conflict within his family. Such distress can be true for us as well if we adopt the avoidance type of expression in conflict.

Sean came into Syracuse Teen Challenge as a quiet 26 year old. He barely spoke and when he did he had a soft voice. Sean kept to himself and followed the guidelines of the program. One day he met Bill who was loud and not afraid to express himself. By circumstance, they happened to sit next to each other in class. Later, Bill started openly criticizing Sean about how sloppy he looked and that he was not cleaning up his area where they both slept. Finally, in exasperation, Bill told Sean in a harsh voice in front of everyone: "Start shaping up now!" Feeling embarrassed, Sean responded timidly, "I will try."

In the following days, it became apparent that Sean looked to avoid Bill. He sat as far away from him as possible during class and meals. Another time, Bill started talking to him at church and he turned around and walked away. It was becoming obvious that Sean wanted to avoid Bill as much as possible. Bill caught onto this and finally confronted him and asked him, "Why are you avoiding me?" Sean wouldn't answer. The next day Sean left the Teen Challenge program and didn't return.

We see here that Sean was so consumed with fear of conflict that he was unable to face Bill and talk about his anger. Usually, confrontation is very hard for an avoider as they feel most comfortable away from angry situations. Regrettably, this problem will follow Sean for the rest of his life until he learns to confront. Ironically, Sean departed so quickly that he missed my biweekly class at Teen Challenge on *How to Express Your Anger in a Biblical Manner*. I teach in this class how the students can confront each other in a safe environment.

Tim Ursiny discusses the features of the avoider in his book, *The Coward's Guide to Conflict:* "People who withdraw use silence, emotional coldness, and distance as weapons or instruments of protection. At times, they will withdraw in order to punish or manipulate the other person. People can withdraw in order to abandon someone until he will change his behavior. Other times, they withdraw because they feel frightened or helpless to change the situation. On these occasions, their withdrawal is based on despair rather then manipulation." Sean used all these aspects.

As I previously stated, I used withdrawal in my conflicts with my wife over many years. As I grew in my Christian faith, I gained the courage to stay in the conflict and we were able to find resolutions to our problems.

Some recommended steps to overcome this form of expressing conflict are:

Ask God for the words to say in a conflict. God can provide you with the effective words to say for resolution. When I did this, I found that God helped me with the proper words to express myself in my conflicts. I also became less affected when harsh words were spoken in a conflict.

Ask God for courage to face difficult conflicts. If you reach out to God, He will strengthen you with the courage to face your conflicts. As you start to express your needs in a conflict, your courage to continue will grow. A helpful idea is to reserve sufficient time with your spouse or friend when major issues arise.

Realize that working together is so important. Working together as a team can help you resolve major problems that come up. Having two people working on an issue can bring new ideas and approaches. Also, you become unified in your approach, which is particularly helpful with children. All this requires being patient with your spouse and trying to compromise to resolve differences.

Summary:

Conflict. Defined as: "a clash, competition, or mutual interference of opposing forces of ideas or interests." Causes are differences: age, gender, race, values, ideas, etc. It can't be avoided, but we have a choice of conflict expressions.

Use conflict pattern. Use patterns to avoid hurt or win the conflict. Pattern is defined as: "a reliable sample of traits, acts or other observable features characterizing an individual." May use one pattern for offense another for defense. Negative patterns don't resolve conflicts, they only leave frustration and bitterness.

Conflict patterns develop. These patterns develop in early childhood. Tend to follow parents' conflict pattern, which is internalized or "imprinted" on us as children. Determining factors in which pattern is chosen by children:

a. **Close relationship to one parent.** Select their conflict pattern.

b. **Difficult relationship.** Imprint strong, even if we hate the conflict type. Can become a generational curse.

c. **Personalities.** Aggressive children drawn to critical pattern-passive child drawn to avoider or vacillator type.

d. **Conflict pattern that wins conflicts.** We follow successful patterns.

University of Denver Prevention and Relationship Enhancement Program (PREP) studied 135 married couples for 12 years. Two negative conflict patterns:

Escalation or criticism. Uses: shouting, swearing, judgmental and forms of intimidation. May work temporarily with someone afraid of conflict, gives a false sense of control. Used until stopped by someone or God. Escalators are: prideful, have weak self-esteem, lack humility, refuse help, deny their issues, are direct, and uncompassionate. Escalators use threats: leaving marriage, firing, not giving love or not talking. Criticizer's goal is to win the conflict. Other characteristics are: stretch the truth, withhold information, and don't listen or try to understand others.

Small irritations are escalated into major battles using harsh words (Proverbs 12:18). Results are: diminished trust and spouses stop revealing themselves. Biblical example David in 2 Samuel 16:5-13. Nonverbal escalation: rolling eyes, throwing up hands, and muttering. All reflect disapproval and shows real feelings. To change, develop: patience, respect, listen and understand the other person.

Withdrawal or Avoidance. Has fear of conflict. Usually a quiet person who: doesn't feel safe in conflict, wants to get away, and struggles to voice own needs. Avoiders have internal anger at the other person and themselves. They use passive-aggressive anger, avoid difficult issues, use denial as defense, don't face problems, and have difficulty resolving conflict. Ironically they may marry a critic, so chaos reigns.

Withdraw to: punish or manipulate, to force a behavior change, are frightened. To change withdrawal: gain courage, ask God for strength and stay in the conflict.

Discussion Questions

1. Are you having a conflict now? Are you able to find resolution?

2. Name one cause of a conflict pattern. Do you use a conflict pattern?

3. Do you use escalation in your conflict(s)? What kind of results do you get?

4. Have you used avoidance or withdrawal in your conflict(s)? Were you pleased with the results?

Chapter 12
Conflict Patterns: Invalidation and Negative Interpretation

The last two negative conflict patterns are:

Invalidation. This is where someone consistently demeans your ideas, feelings and even yourself. They use belittling tactics and words to win the conflict and force their ideas onto you and others. Their words are designed to hurt and to intimidate, such as: "You don't know what you are talking about" and "If only I could be perfect like you." Moreover, non-verbal actions are employed such as: ignoring the person talking, not looking directly at the person, and being critical of the other person with others in public. All these actions reflect a profound disrespect for the receiving person and usually lead to negative retaliation.

Each incident cuts to the heart of the receiver and the former trust and closeness deteriorates with each attack. The irony is that when one starts using this expression in a conflict, the other frequently responds using invalidation or another one of the negative conflict patterns. Consequently, each party drives the other apart even faster. In a marriage, at this stage, they start to wonder where their original mutual love and care went, as the relationship feels so painful now. Roy Milam in his article, *Why Marriages Fail: Invalidation (Part 2 of 4)*, states that: "Invalidation is one of the most serious communication mistakes spouses can make in their marriage, in how they respond to each other . . . An overt caustic remark may even convey a sense of contempt of the other partner for another." Such invalidation was played out in this true situation.

Emily met Joe when they were in their early twenties. There was such an electricity when they were together. Their strong physical attraction to each other soon led them to become sexually active before their quick marriage. They spent little time talking over their dreams and values. Consequently, the relationship had not developed into a personal friendship before their marriage.

Emily noticed that Joe had a way of jesting that put down her fear of the dark. When she was young she had been frightened by the dark by some other kids and that had left a painful memory. Thinking that "true love conquers all things" she felt they would work this out later. Soon after the marriage, however, Joe's comments about her concerns of coping with dark places became more sarcastic and biting to her. She felt such pain in her heart after one of their interchanges that she started crying. Joe's cold response was for her "to get over it." As a mode of self-protection, she started to withdraw from him and would not discuss her painful fears with him. Instead, she talked these issues over with her girl friend, Sue.

In retaliation, Emily became less responsive to Joe's constant sexual advances. He, in turn, increased his acerbic comments asking her. "Did you forget your responsibility as a wife to sexually love me?" Naturally, this approach didn't win Emily over and soon she was fighting back with her own invalidating comments. Their battles increased in intensity and length and were very evident to their two young children. The shouting and demeaning went on for hours as each tried to hurt the other with more painful remarks.

It was like a contest where nothing was ever resolved. Finally, each in exhaustion, they would retreat to their own separate rooms since they were now sleeping apart. Each spent time plotting revenge with even more caustic comments against the other. Each, because of using invalidation, had unknowingly descended into bitterness, and eventually they were divorced.

The invalidation that Joe and Emily expressed is discussed in Kerby Anderson's article, *Why Marriages Fail,* shows how: ". . . invalidation can also be much more subtle. It may involve an argument where contempt for the other partner is so obvious. One partner may merely be putting the other partner down for his or her feelings." Besides their mistaken use of invalidation, both Emily and Joe had the additional limitation of not knowing Christ or His Word. Therefore, they didn't know 1 Peter 3:9, which says: *"Do not repay evil with evil or insult with insult, but with blessing, because to this you were called so that you might inherit a blessing."* Thus, if Emily and Joe had sought God and professional help, they might have recognized their problem and changed from this deadly pattern. They also missed the opportunity to turn to positive conflict.

To correct the use of invalidation in your conflicts, do the following:

Identify that you are using invalidation in your conflict expression. Pray to God to convict you that you are using invalidation with your spouse or friend.

Look for and verbally appreciate the positive characteristics of your spouse. Remember them, when some of the irritating characteristics arise in the relationship. Also affirm your spouse/friend by telling them of their strengths.

Try to show love by providing a safe, nonjudgmental atmosphere. Establish such safety by providing privacy when discussing difficult issues. It is most important to be non-judgmental in your comments of your spouse/friend. Remember when giving advice, do not put the person down, but correct their actions. Such an atmosphere encourages the discussion of difficult subjects. Tell your spouse/friend of your willingness to discuss those topics, which have been difficult to discuss in the past.

Use active listening. Paying attention to the words the spouse/ friend is saying and their emotions. When you do, you are better able to understand the real message of the other person and respond in an understanding manner. Furthermore, you are able to repeat the ideas and emotions back to the speaker, which shows them that you understand them. This step builds trust between the parties.

Negative interpretation. This is when you constantly believe that the motives and ideas of a spouse or friend are more negative than they truly are. Negative interpretation is really belief in a lie (my spouse is out to get me), which determines our decisions, and in turn our actions or comments. We don't realize that it is a lie, so we proceed as if it were the truth. When this involves our spouse or friend, we are consistently alienating them, creating division in the relationship. Some examples are: "I know you don't like what I said" even before you have replied, or "You don't like my new hair style, do you?" When there is increased stress in the relationship, the probability of negative interpretation arises in conflicts in an interpersonal relationship.

Negative interpretation is thinking everyone, including your spouse or dear friend, is thinking negatively of you and your performance, which often is the opposite from the truth. Frequently, this is a legacy from a childhood where you received mostly negative comments on your looks, actions and achievements. You developed a mind-set to expect such negative reactions from everyone about you and your performance. As a self-protection, you mistakenly thought you could reduce the sting of these put-downs by being the first one to express these negative thoughts to the other person. It seemed that by speaking these negative opinions about yourself diminished their power. Ironically, you would later discover, what you thought was not the truth.

Sometimes a wife wants a fast answer from her husband on what she considers a pressing concern or action. Her husband may take longer to process the issue in his mind. This difference in processing can easily lead to negative interpretation on the wife's part. She might think: *Perhaps he does not want (motive) to help me.* Many times the opposite is true. Other times, the situation is reversed. Learning to recognize and honor the processing times of your mate or friend is so important for the emotional health of a relationship. Kerby Anderson in his article, *Why Marriages Fail,* confirms the significance of processing times: "Learning to understand and respect the processing times of your mate or friend is important for the relationship. Negative interpretations do not change easily."

Negative interpretations involve the subtlety of many nonverbal expressions such as "rolling of one's eyes " at something they think is strange. Other nonverbal examples may include: grimaces, scowls, shrugging of shoulders, etc. They are so subtle to recognize that many people miss them entirely. Yet, men use them frequently as their main means of communicating negative thoughts. How to react back to them in a positive Christian way is also challenging. The real story below demonstrates the dangers of negative interpretations.

Leslie was a quiet yet friendly person who had grown up with a strict mother who controlled her actions. Also, her mother wanted her to be upbeat and positive so she didn't allow Leslie to express negative comments about herself or her feelings. It was as if there was a "pollyanna" atmosphere in the home. To express her true feelings, Leslie learned to employ nonverbal negative interpretations, especially rolling her eyes and sighing as signs of her disapproval. Later, she learned to use verbal negative interpretations as this expression seemed to fit her withdrawn personality.

Leslie carried this habit into her marriage with Cliff, who soon learned to identify and partially understand her nonverbal communication. One of the major problems with all nonverbal communication is that it usually communicates disapproval without the clarity of words. Cliff thought, *What exactly do these nonverbals mean?* In their conflicts, Leslie would use both verbal and nonverbal expression. She would constantly question Cliff with "Do you really love me?" Cliff responded, "Yes, I do love you. Don't you realize that by now?"

Also he tried to show her how much he loved her, but he lacked some of the verbal skills to fully express his love. He would work diligently at the tasks she gave him as a means of demonstrating his love for her, but Leslie didn't seem to recognize his efforts. Often, she would demean what he did and hardly ever affirm Cliff for his attempts to show his love for her. These tactics left Cliff feeling frustrated, angry and unloved. Eventually he erupted into rage at her. The marriage relationship became very rocky and ended sadly in divorce.

A cycle developed between the spouses with each expressing their conflict in their own negative way. The difficult part is that neither spouse was able to identify and take steps to correct their negative conflict patterns. Continued repeated frustration eventually leads one onto the path to bitterness.

To counter the use of negative interpretations in our lives, we need to:

Pray to God to gain His direction on the situation. Review our beliefs and actions of our spouse or friend. Are you really being objective about the other person? 2 Corinthians 10:5 states: ". . . *take every thought captive and make it obedient to Christ.*"

Are they really trying their best? Is there anything positive that they are saying or doing? Remember that sincere effort reflects true motives. Maybe the other person just can't perform at the level you expect, but remember that works both ways (see the section in Chapter 2 on expectations).

Observe the actions and words of your mate or friend. See if any of your conclusions about them could be mistaken. Try to find positive evidence to the contrary to your negative interpretations of your spouse or friend. Then evaluate this new evidence compared to your original conclusions. Were you mistaken in your original determination? Pray to God for wisdom to understand the truth.

Gradually substitute your new truth(s) in your interactions with the other person. Observe the positive change(s) that you see in your spouse/friend and affirm them on those changes. If you both affirm each other about these positive changes, there will be fewer negative conflicts in the relationship. Remember Philippians 4:6-7: *"Do not be anxious about anything, but in everything by prayer and petition, with thanksgiving, present your requests to God. And the peace of God, which transcends all understanding, will guard your hearts and minds in Christ Jesus."*

We have seen the damaging effects of using invalidation and negative interpretations on relationships. They are part of Satan's plan to divide us as couples and friends and to lead us into becoming bitter in spirit. It is important that we recognize these dangers and stop these negative forms of conflict especially in our most important relationships.

Summary:

Invalidation. This is when someone demeans your ideas, feelings and even you as a person. Invalidators belittle you to win and force their ideas on you. They use nonverbal actions such as: ignore you and not look at you. These reflect disrespect and leads to retaliation. The invalidator employs caustic comments, which cuts the spouse's heart and destroys trust. The receiving spouse may take revenge using invalidation. These actions drive people apart (1Peter 3:9).

To correct: identify invalidation, validate spouse's feelings and ideas, provide comfort for spouse, and create more safety to open up.

Negative Interpretation. We believe our spouse's motives are more negative than they really are. They act on a lie and feel their spouse is out to get them. They constantly alienate their spouse, which creates a divided relationship.

Negative interpretation develops in childhood where many of us received negative comments on: looks, actions and achievements. We then may expect negative reactions from everyone. As a self-protection we may begin to express negative comments about ourselves to others. The difference between genders in processing time depends on the issue.

To correct: Pray for wisdom, look for positives in spouse, examine conclusions of the spouse, are they mistaken? Substitute your new truth(s) in your relationship.

Discussion Questions

1. What is the invalidation form of conflict? Do you use it?
Are you happy with the results?

2. Describe negative interpretation. Have you ever used it in your conflicts?

3. If you use negative interpretations, would you want to try the steps to correct this pattern?

Chapter 13
Conflict Pattern Styles

Besides the different types of conflict, there are also different styles of conflict patterns that use many of the types of conflict discussed in the last chapter. These styles may involve two or more participants. Some characteristics of negative styles include: not listening to the other person or trying to understand their position. Each party just wants to reaffirm his/her position. Also, each party has pride in their position, as both want to win, so there is no desire for compromise between the parties. Instead, each wants to control the conflict on their own terms. Accordingly, they pursue a negative style which never finds resolution creating frustration that develops into bitterness.

These styles are as follows:

The circular pattern. When two people argue using one of the negative types of conflict expression, they become locked in a style pattern of conflict that goes round and round with no resolution. Hence the title, circular pattern, is a shape that has no end. Each party learns to anticipate the other's words and actions and develops a counter-defensive reaction. Even though they abhor this pattern, they often don't know how to get out of it. Many even learn to feel comfortable in the pattern and live with the irritation. Still many others become so frustrated, it leads to resentment, which quickly becomes bitterness. If one of the parties tries to break out of the pattern, the other often strongly counters to re-establish the pattern. These counter moves include hostile comments and manipulation to retain the original pattern. Ironically, many people find comfort in the familiarity of staying in the pattern. Even if it is frustrating, they know what to expect.

Some examples of this style of conflict are:

a. Parent-child. Where one spouse or friend is responsible, "adult-like," in his/her behavior and the other is "child-like" and irresponsible. Both participants seem to accept their roles because of their own personal characteristics. Despite this acceptance, each is irritated in their roles. The "adult" person gets frustrated at having to constantly deal with the helplessness and negligence of the "child." At the same time, the "child" feels demeaned by the criticism and control exercised by the "adult." Thus, they develop a circular conflict that finally ends with one, usually the "child," withdrawing in tears or anger.

Meanwhile, the "adult" feels stuck in the situation. Both are ripe to develop bitterness. Dr. Bill Mitcham, therapist, in his article in the Mooresville Tribune entitled, *Breaking Destructive Patterns a Key to Couple Conflict Resolution,* states: "One common marital pattern between marriage partners is the parent-child syndrome. This marital dance is when one spouse over-functions and the other one under-functions." He goes on to say: "It is a waste of time to argue, if he wasn't so over controlling, she would act less like a child or if she wasn't so childlike, he wouldn't have to take over and make all the major decisions. To correct the bad marital dance, both spouses need to begin interacting as two mature adults and break the parent/child pattern. Both have to change and stop the blame game."

b. The emotion pursuer/emotional avoider pattern. Here the pursuer tries to share his/her emotions of a situation with the avoider to reduce their anxiety. On the other hand, the avoider uses withdrawal and reasoning to handle the same situation. If they hold to their positions, these polar opposites create a negative conflict pattern.

Usually the pursuer attacks the avoider for being "unfeeling" and unable to meet his/her needs for talk and comfort. The avoider responds with logic and intellectual arguments purposely avoiding the emotions. Neither of the participants really wants to listen or understand the other as each lives in their own world. Each uses this pattern to avoid facing the reality of their world. Consequently, nothing is settled causing irritation with bitterness starting to form.

Harriett Lerner, PhD, in her book, *The Dance of Anger,* states: "Emotional pursuers protect emotional distancers. By doing the work of expressing the neediness, clingingness, and wish for closeness for both partners, pursuers make it possible for distancers to avoid confronting their own dependency wishes and insecurities." Later, she describes the way out of this seeming dilemma: "When a pursuer learns to back off and put her energies into her own life—especially if she can do this with dignity into her own life and *without hostility*—the distancer is more likely to recognize his own needs for contact and closeness."

Sean, in his late teens, met Carol and was highly attracted to her. They had a fast courtship marked with intense sexual feelings for each other. There had been little discussion of values and goals before they got married within six months. Soon after the marriage, they discovered that Carol was an emotional pursuer while Sean was an emotional avoider. Their arguments started with Carol intensely pursuing Sean on some issue that concerned her or something that she wanted. Sean would struggle to avoid her. He just wanted to have peace in the relationship, so usually he would submit to her requests. His quiet submission only led to her openly demeaning him to her family and friends, saying: "Sean will not talk with me." These actions strongly diminished their initial close intimacy, leaving each feeling more isolated and in pain.

This circular dance of conflict never resulted in any resolution. Instead it created an increased urge by Sean to escape, while Carol pushed even harder for Sean to talk about his emotions. To escape this torment, Sean turned to drugs and fled the house. He was eventually found by a relative who convinced him to go to Teen Challenge for help. There he learned, in my class, Anger and Conflict, how to express anger in a godly way, and to stay in the conflict. Armed with this new approach, Sean was able to confront Carol in a new way. Carol pushed back with the old negative ways with insults and anger. He asked her to go with him to counseling but she refused. Regrettably the marriage ended in divorce, but Sean went to counseling and is now more content and confident when conflict arises.

We see in this narrative the destructive power of the circular pattern in two lives. Nonetheless, there is hope to break such a pattern as follows:

Recognize that a circular pattern is occurring in your conflicts. Negative anger is usually expressed causing your emotions to take over the conflict. You do not find any resolution in your conflicts. Instead, you both stay stuck in your original positions.

Pray to God to change this dynamic and guide you. He will help you to change your role in the conflict. Furthermore, He will calm down your emotions and allow you to find a new way of listening and expressing yourself.

If you are a pursuer, stop the pursuit. Let the other person experience their emotions in the situation. If you are the pursued, ask God to help you to stay in the conflict and not be afraid to express your emotions with your partner.

For the adult/child pattern, both parties need to try to change. Both parties need to be responsible and respectful of each other. The child needs to take small steps of responsible adult behavior. It is important for the adult to give encouragement, not criticism, to the child for every responsible step they take.

Commit to establish a new positive conflict pattern. Try to work together with God's direction to find solutions to resolving your problems. Use the positive conflict approach in Chapter 14. Read Psalms, particularly 22, 23, 27 and 31 to give you hope and help with your emotions in a time of trial.

Both parties using negative interpretation or invalidation. When these negative patterns are used by one or both parties, they often lead to a circular conflict. One party needs to take the initiative by not using either of these two negative expressions. In its place, that same person starts acting respectfully towards the other party. Encourage the other person to drop their negative expression in favor of a positive pattern.

The triangle pattern. This is when we transfer most of our emotions from our spouse to another party as a way of reducing our anxiety. Such apprehension is a product of unresolved conflicts in our main relationship. Also, the third party appears to provide the missing support and affirmation lacking in our primary relationship. We bring the issues of our conflict(s) to the third person, who is a friend with a sympathetic ear. They will agree with us and make us feel better. Other times the third person may be of the opposite gender so a destructive sexual relationship may develop that destroys the marriage relationship. In any case, emotionally bringing in a third party never solves the basic problems in the primary relationship and only delays resolution, which can end in divorce and bitterness.

Harriett Lerner, PhD, describes in her book, *The Dance of Anger*, the different types of triangle relationships: ". . . triangles take many forms. On a transient basis triangles operate automatically and unconsciously in all human contexts including our family, our work setting, and our friendship networks. But triangles can become rigidly entrenched, blocking the growth of the individuals in them keeping us from identifying the actual sources of conflict in our relationships." As Harriett Lerner points out, we all get involved in triangles on a temporary basis as a means of finding comfort from a friend over a conflict. As long as the emotional intensity is not shifted to this secondary relationship, such a temporary triangle can actually help the conflict by bringing both support and new helpful ideas. It is when the person's emotional health becomes dependent upon this third person, that the triangle becomes ingrained and trouble begins in the primary relationship.

Ray met Ellen when they were in their early twenties. They married after one year and within six years had three children. Their conflicts usually were started by Ellen pursuing Ray as he would withdraw. In her emotional intensity, Ellen would say, "I just want to talk with you" but Ray, feeling her intense emotions, would leave the room. This action would leave Ellen extremely frustrated because she needed a listening ear and solace for her trials.

Ellen, feeling Ray was not meeting her critical need(s), was looking to unload her pent-up emotions with someone who would listen and empathize with her. During a shopping trip, she accidentally met an old friend, Robin. During their conversation, Ellen could feel Robin listening and providing emotional support to her. Gradually a strong connection developed and soon they were having coffee together regularly. Ellen had found the sympathetic person that she had desperately sought. Trust quickly developed with Robin and before long Ellen discussed her deepest feelings about her marriage. She found herself pouring out years of frustration with Ray. Robin would listen and seem so understanding of Ellen's hurt. Also, Robin gave Ellen advice on how to deal with her relationship with Ray. Ellen kept her relationship with Robin secret from Ray as she thought that he could stay in his own world.

Meanwhile, the irritations between them were not being resolved and anger kept bubbling up in the relationship. Gradually, Ellen increased her meetings with Robin and soon a rigid triangle had been formed. Meanwhile, Ray was feeling even more distant from his wife.

In retaliation, Ray went out with his buddies to a bar and met a girl, Angie, who attracted him. She seemed so pleasant and calm without the intensity of Ellen. Before long, he was seeing Angie more frequently and started talking about his constant irritations with Ellen. In effect, a double triangle had been created. As these triangles went on, the marriage began to die and sadly they also ended up divorced.

Thus, we see the dangers of triangles in a marriage and the necessity of both parties to try harder, with God's help, to work out their issues together.

In Genesis 27, we see such a triangle between Isaac and his wife Rebekah and their sons Jacob and Esau. Isaac wants to bless his oldest son Esau, but: *"Now Rebekah was listening as Isaac spoke to his son Esau . . ."* Rebekah said to Jacob: *"'Now my son, listen carefully and do what I tell you: Go out to the flock and bring me two choice young goats, so I can prepare some tasty food for your father, just the way he likes it. Then take it to your father to eat, so that he may give you his blessing before he dies.'"* Here we see Rebekah plotting with her son, Jacob, to deceive her husband and son, Esau, out of Esau's rightful blessing due him as the oldest son. Rebekah had always favored Jacob, as Isaac had favored Esau, resulting in both setting up destructive triangles with their children. Instead of confronting her husband, she uses deceit to get her way. Such a harmful action leads to a breakup of the family. Jacob has to flee the wrath of his brother over his deception, and Rebekah never sees Jacob again. Such can be the destructiveness of triangles in a relationship.

The technique to correct a triangle conflict is as follows:

Identify that a triangle pattern is going on in your relationship. Look for the signs of a triangle in your relationship(s) by seeing if your spouse or friend discusses their emotional or important issues with you. If you have started a triangle yourself, make a commitment to break it.

Seek God's direction of how to change from a triangle pattern.
God will give you the courage and words to say when you face your
primary party with your issues. Be aware that the strongest triangles start in your immediate family. Beware of crossing generational lines, like telling one of your children your problems with
your spouse. The children can find out the truth for themselves.

Discuss the existence of the triangle with your spouse. Either
partner's needs may cause that party to bring up the topic. Let the
party, who is outside the triangle, discuss how it isolates him/her.
Ask the spouse to leave the triangle and to try again to talk and listen to their partner's concerns. The partner, in the triangle, needs
to discuss their reasons why they are in the triangle. Then they need
to try to detach from it and give the main relationship another chance
at meeting their needs. Remember praying together builds not only
your mutual spiritual life, but your sense of unity. It has proven in
my life to greatly help me and my spouse in times of conflict.

If you are the third person in a triangle, try to disengage. This
action involves stopping the following: giving advice, being the
sole emotional refuge and agreeing that all the blame lies with the
other party in the primary relationship. In effect, you become
more neutral. Stay supportive but nonjudgmental. Advise the
other person to start talking directly with the primary party to
seek true resolution. The primary partners need to work out their
issues together and, if needed, meet with a Christian therapist.
Remember, that this process will take time and patience. Be aware
that one of the parties may try to re-establish the triangle because
they feel so accustomed to it.

If these steps fail. Persevere in redoing steps 1-3 until your confidence in resolving conflict(s) together without a third party
becomes more secure.

Negative Generational pattern. This starts when a negative conflict style, modeled by a father/mother, is adopted by their sons and/or daughters, who in turn pass that same conflict style on to their children. An example of a negative generational conflict pattern occurs when an aggressive, angry father consistently shouts and curses at his children. They fear and hate what he is doing. However, because of the power of this negative modeling (imprinting), the children end up repeating the same curse on their own children. Such a pattern becomes replayed countless times, as it seems to automatically pass down through the generations. Finally, an adult, realizing the harm being inflicted, elects to change from this negative pattern to a positive conflict pattern for the sake of his children and himself. This change process is hard as I can attest to in my own life.

> My father, when I was learning to drive, would constantly try to correct my driving. Even after I received my driving license, he would correct me, much to my frustration. One time when I was driving the family car and he started correcting my every move, I said to him in aggravation: "I'm stopping here. You drive!" I went on to tell him of my utter frustration with his unrelenting corrections. As a result, he ended up driving.
>
> Later, when I was teaching my teenage son to drive, I was surprised to hear the same corrective words of my father coming from my mouth. My compulsion to repeat the same "curse" was that strong. I vowed to change and literally held my hand over my mouth to prevent me from repeating my father's curse.

In his book, *The Anger Trap*, Dr. Les Carter writes about the generational conflict pattern: "In an extremely high percentage of cases involving people who create pain by the misuse of anger, the generations preceding them mishandled anger too. Since learning is accomplished through modeling, the lessons a developing child receives can become the foundation for later behavior and unless a determination is made to take a healthier approach, troublesome patterns remain." I have seen in my five year old granddaughter how quickly she is adopting the habits of her parents. For children, conflict between their parents can be a frightening experience, so the child seeks to find what he/she thinks is a "safe" way to express angry feelings. As the child grows up, he/she seeks to find their own way of handling conflict. Often they will experiment with different types of conflict types until they settle on one which feels most comfortable.

The Bible speaks to the negative generational pattern in Exodus 34:7: *"Yet he does not leave the guilty unpunished; he punishes the children and their children for the sin of the fathers to the third and fourth generation."* We have to remember that unresolved anger develops into bitterness, which is a sin. Consequently, we unknowingly will find that our inability to resolve conflict can easily create an ongoing painful pattern that spreads throughout our family for succeeding generations. This conflict style has such a long-term destructive effect that it needs to be addressed. We can, with God's help, turn around this negative conflict pattern for good by starting what I call a "generational blessing." As Deuteronomy 7: 9 states: *"Know therefore that the Lord your God is God; he is the faithful God, keeping his covenant of love to a thousand generations of those who love him and keep his commands."* Expressing positive conflict can initiate a legacy of blessing for our children and grandchildren. First, we need to stop any negative conflict pattern that we are using.

> William brought not only his family but his hostile anger from Northern Ireland to America. He was known for his loud shouting and verbal conflicts with the family. His son, also named William, hated these conflicts between his parents and vowed to handle his conflicts differently. Little did he realize that his father's anger expression had become ingrained into his psyche.
>
> After William got married, he found that the pressures of married life plus his wife's irritations got to him emotionally. Soon, he too, not knowing any alternative, fell into resorting

to the same angry expressions as his father. William's family suffered like he had but the deadly seed had been planted and now the generational curse had begun. Even though the family went to church regularly and read the Bible occasionally, they never had a "born again" experience. Thus, the family was spiritually shallow and continued to be burdened by the curse of negative conflict. In some latter generations, alcoholism was taken up by the fathers, which left the mothers struggling to fulfill both father and mother roles.

Finally in the ninth generation a son, a "born again" Christian, hated the curse and sought a different approach. He studied anger and conflict and learned that with God's direction that he had a choice of what type of conflict he used. Consequently, he rejected his father's deadly imprint and changed to the "blessing of positive conflict." That is my story and I pray that my son will continue the "blessing."

To heal negative generational conflict and start a generational blessing, do the following:

Realize that you have a negative conflict, generational pattern. This acknowledgement is the important first step. Even though you may have detested this imprint, you realize that you now have a choice to change this deadly pattern to a positive model. Your bitter conflict pattern may now be infecting your children with the curse. Stop now and change to a positive pattern, before they extend the curse.

Pray to God for help. You need His guidance and strength in changing from the negative to positive conflict pattern. He can guide you on the right path of change. Remember, you have the choice to stay with the curse from your parents or change it to a "blessing" for subsequent generations.

Discuss and model it with your spouse and children. Explain that you, and hopefully your spouse, will now be using positive conflict instead of negative conflict. You will need to explain the positive conflict process, as described in the next chapter, to your spouse and children. Most important is you are modeling positive conflict vs. your former negative approach. Such modeling proves that you are serious and provides the positive imprint the children seek. Remember that change usually doesn't happen immediately but with time, God's direction, and persistence. Tell them how you feel better with this new approach to conflict compared to how you felt before.

If your children have already adopted your negative conflict style. Talk to them about how you changed to a positive style that works. Explain to them why you needed to change from the constant strife of your former negative conflict style. Now you feel more peace in your life and you are resolving your conflicts. Encourage them that they can to do the same with God's help.

Persevere using positive conflict. This form of conflict is discussed completely in the next chapter.

As we have seen, there are many ways in which we can easily become entangled with different styles of negative conflict patterns. Because of their lack of respect, pain inflicted and lack of resolution, negative conflict patterns often lead us onto the path toward bitterness. God sees our anguish from being on such a path and wants to help us. Now that we are aware of these patterns, it is our responsibility to commit to change. With God's guidance and direction, we can succeed and go down a godly path using positive conflict.

Summary:

Conflict Pattern Styles. Defined as two or more participants using negative styles. These styles are:

The circular pattern. When two people argue using negative conflict expression. Characteristics are: stuck in the pattern, goes around with no resolution. Each party anticipates other's words and actions, and develops counter-defensive reactions. They may hate pattern but don't know how to get out and feel comfortable in pattern, but become frustrated in it. If one tries to break the pattern, the other tries to keep pattern. Examples are:

a. Parent-child. One spouse is responsible, "adult-like" other is "child- like" and irresponsible. Both dislike their roles: the "adult" gets frustrated with the helplessness of the "child." The "child" feels demeaned.

To correct: the "child" needs to become more responsible.

b. Emotion pursuer-emotional avoider. The pursuer tries to share their emotions with avoider who withdraws.

To break a circular pattern: recognize it, ask God for help. Pursuer stops pursuing. Establish a new positive pattern.

Triangle pattern. Occurs when one transfers their emotions from a primary relationship to third party to reduce anxiety. Brings issues of primary conflict to the other party for a sympathetic ear. Focuses on telling other spouse's fault(s). to third party (Genesis 27).

Everyone has temporary triangles for comfort and they can help with new ideas. Problems arise when emotions shift from the primary relationship.

To break triangle pattern: recognize it, pray for God's help, start discussing issues with primary partner and allow family members to develop their own relationship with other members. If you are the third party in a triangle, try to detach, stop giving advice, become neutral, stay supportive but suggest the person talk directly with their primary party.

Negative Generational pattern. This pattern begins when negative conflict is modeled by a parent and adopted by his children who pass it to their children. This continues through generations until an adult stops it (Exodus 34:7).

To heal generational conflict: realize it and the strong inclination to follow it, ask God's direction, start using positive pattern.

Discussion Questions

1. Have you ever been involved in a circular conflict pattern? Did you find resolution?

2. Are you currently using a triangle pattern for your conflicts? Are you pleased with the results?

3. How do you break a triangle conflict pattern?

4. Is your family in a negative generational pattern? How do you change it to a generational blessing?

Chapter 14
The Power of Positive Conflict

In the last three chapters, we have seen how negative conflict pattern types and styles can gradually lead us into bitterness and broken relationships. These patterns fail because they lack the fundamental biblical principles that are necessary to reach the successful resolution of difficult issues. In addition, these patterns are marked by disrespect in both words and actions. They are used by each of the parties to gain advantage, or as a means of self-protection. Our goal should be to achieve mutual resolution between the parties, which requires caring words and a kindly approach. These godly principles in order of importance are:

Seeking God's help. Instead of proceeding in our own strength, it is critically important that we seek God's help through prayer for wisdom, direction, and calmness. Paul in 1 Corinthians 1:25 speaks to this: *"For the foolishness of God is wiser than man's wisdom, and the weakness of God is stronger than man's strength."* Often in a conflict, we let our emotions control our speaking and actions to our detriment. By developing a daily relationship with God through our Bible reading and prayer, we are ready and able to receive His calming guidance on how to speak and what words to say when the need arises.

Establishing a safe atmosphere for mutual communication. We must feel safe, physically and emotionally, to be able to act and to express our opinions and feelings. This type of safety is defined as: "exemption from hurt, injury, or loss." Here differences between the parties can be revealed without the retaliation of physical hurt or emotional put-downs. Safety is critical, as reaffirmed by Howard Markman, Scott Stanley & Susan Blumberg, in their book, *Fighting for Your Marriage:*

"Positive connections and intimacy thrive when things are safe—when you are confident that you can do your part to control conflicts." The writers go on: "When you have the skills to handle conflicts, you are able to relax, to be yourself, and to open the doors to emotional and physical intimacy." Such a safe atmosphere encourages greater freedom of expression for both parties and less negative conflict. Both parties are now able to seek mutual understanding and achieve reconciliation. This goal is reflective of an attitude of care for the other person and a respect for their ideas that enrich the whole relationship.

Such true safety is only found in the Lord's provision, as found in Proverbs 29:25: *"Fear of man will prove to be a snare, but whoever trusts in the Lord is kept safe."* Also in Psalm 27:5: *"For in the day of trouble he will keep me safe in his dwelling; he will hide me in the shelter of his tabernacle and set me high upon a rock."* When both parties trust in Him, He will develop the safe place that they so desperately seek.

When such safety as described above is missing, the hurt party fears revealing their true thoughts, which prevents resolution. Instead, the hurt party wants to escape the abuse. Often, they will plot revenge against the person endangering them.

We usually use the word "confronting" someone when we are in conflict. I want to change that word for positive conflict to "carefronting." By "carefronting," we show care for the other person in our conflict through respectful words and actions. By showing kindness in this way, the other person will usually respond in a more respectful manner in return. Also, these steps help us achieve resolution, or at least much greater understanding of the other person's positions or ideas. This call for respect is highlighted in 1 Peter 2: *"Show proper respect to everyone: Love the brotherhood of believers, fear God, honor the king."* Respect in positive conflict needs to be demonstrated in the following ways:

Speaking in a calm tone. The initial tone of the speaker's voice can often affect, positively or negatively, the outcome of the conflict and whether it will be resolved or not. When someone speaks calmly to us, we feel their respect. They appear to be looking for positive resolution. As Proverbs 15:1 states: *"A gentle answer turns away wrath, but a harsh word stirs up anger."* Thus, employing a loud voice in a conflict will too often result in the recipient responding in similar fashion, only intensifying the conflict.

Using positive words. The words we use have vast power to help or hurt our exchanges. Proverbs 12:18 addresses this: *"Reckless words pierce like a sword, but the tongue of the wise brings healing."* Using positive words will greatly encourage resolution, while negative words have the opposite effect. In her book, *The Power of Positive Confrontation,* Barbara Pachter reaffirms this: **"Avoid harsh adjectives and descriptive words when describing the other person's behavior.** ... Avoid other harsh words like 'disgusting,' 'lazy,' 'selfish,' 'revolting,' and 'annoying.' These have the same effect as negative words—they put the other person on the defensive. If that happens, the chances of having a positive confrontation aren't so good." Other words that can be damaging include: always, never, absolutely, etc, which usually aren't true. These absolutes imply that the recipient is very delinquent in his or her responsibilities. Therefore, before we speak our words, we need to think out their effect on the other person. If you are angry with what someone did, talk to them about their hurtful actions, not about them as a person. For example: "I was angry with you when you didn't call me to tell me that you couldn't meet with me." vs. "You are so lazy. You never call me when you aren't coming to our meeting." Such painful generalizations are demeaning and so unclear that they destroy the basis for resolution.

Also, remember to use "I" statements, not "you" statements. For example: "I was hurt when you said I was so stupid." A hurtful approach would be: "You show how dumb you are when you call me stupid." Using "I" statements softens the harshness of the message, especially when it is an accusation. Barbara Pachter in her book supports this: "'I' statements are usually assertive statements. 'You' statements encourage blame and generalizations. 'I' statements will encourage you to keep the emphasis on yourself. Remember, 'You' can put people on the defensive." Negative conflict is often times marked by the parties putting each other down using "you" statements as a form of attack on the other.

Listening closely to the words spoken and the emotions shown. You need to listen carefully enough to the speaker's words, so that you would be able to repeat them exactly (called reflective listening). This procedure is necessary if you are going to clearly understand what the other person is proposing. Then, if you don't clearly understand them, you are able to ask clarifying questions.

Misunderstandings are commonplace in negative conflict causing the conflict to escalate and become drawn-out. If we consider conflict is an opportunity to understand each other, we need to take the necessary time to speak clearly about what we really want to say to each other. Everyone longs to be understood. This step is so important for our attaining successful resolution of conflicts. Remember, listening to a person does not necessarily mean agreeing with them. James 1:19 affirms the importance of listening: ". . . *Everyone should be quick to listen, slow to speak and slow to become angry.*" Also in Proverbs 10:19: " *When words are many, sin is not absent, but he who holds his tongue is wise.*" Notice, in both verses, the emphasis is on listening first before talking. By careful listening you show respect toward the other person, thereby creating a greater desire in them to listen to your position. Also, be aware of conflicting non-verbal expressions such as: rolling of eyes, looking away, or shaking of the head, etc.

People communicate their true meaning through several different ways including: words, emotions and non-verbal actions. When all of these are sending the same message, the communication is clear. Unfortunately, this does not always happen, especially in negative conflict. We say one thing, but confuse the meaning by expressing it with contradictory emotions. I can happily say, "I'm

OK," but show a depressed body language so that the real meaning is confused. Our emotions often convey the truth more than the words we say. As a result, if a message seems confusing between the words and emotions, it is important for us to first determine the other person's emotions.

> Shelly was the youngest of five daughters. As she grew up, she felt issues intensely and found that she could discuss these feelings with her mother, who favored her. For hours, she would vent her emotions with her mother who would listen intently. Soon, going to her mother became Shelly's frequent habit to release these pent-up frustrations. She felt relieved that someone would listen to her. The problem, however, was she only wanted to talk and not listen for helpful advice. Consequently, she developed a headstrong manner of wanting only her way.
>
> Jack came into Shelly's life after high school. They dated and soon were married. Jack also was strong-willed and loud when he talked. Initially, he listened to Shelly's complaints, but gradually got very frustrated with her constant complaints. Jack would say to her, "Why won't you at least try my suggestion and not just reject it." Jack's frustration grew as Shelly continued to go her own self-centered way. Gradually, their conflicts got worse, as each side became stuck in their positions. Painfully, they got divorced. Shelly, to this day, still wants you to listen to her, but usually will not listen to you.

What was missing from Shelly's communication was the desire to have dialogue with the other person. Dialogue is talking, then listening, then talking again without interrupting so that there is a flow of conversation. This process develops a mutual feeling of respect for the other person's words and ideas. In this way, mutual understanding can be achieved and resolution is possible.

Looking the person in their eyes. This action is a natural means of connecting with the other person while talking, especially during a quarrel. Furthermore, when you are looking at them, you are able to read their body language expressions. These non-verbal expressions provide a clue as to the person's real intent. Again, if the words don't match up with the body language, the words probably aren't the true story. Often in negative conflict, the parties don't always look at each other in their eyes. When this happens most people feel disrespected and might wonder if the person is telling them the truth. Conversely, looking into the other person's eyes builds trust making resolution possible.

By showing respect, using the words and actions listed above, we enhance the probability that we too will be respected. I fully realize that it may seem difficult to remember and use all of these respectful steps in the middle of a heated conflict. Therefore, just try using the first two steps and later try the others to see if they didn't help you achieve a positive resolution. Once you have mastered these few steps, then move on to include more.

Expressing your intentions clearly. When you express your needs and desires clearly, this reduces confusion as to what you are seeking. To be successful, we often need to take the time to think out our goals before we talk to someone about them. Author Barbara Pachter, in her book mentioned earlier, encourages us to know exactly what we want the other person to do, and to express it to them. She writes: "If you are not specific in what you ask the other person to do, you may not get what you want. You may get what the other person thinks you want or what the other person wants to do or give." Thus, if you are not specific, you will often end up being disappointed and angry because you think that they are purposely not meeting your need(s). With negative conflict, there is no such pondering because usually passion has taken over. Ironically, it is in these very conflicts where we want to express our intentions clearly.

Face your conflict as a team. Confronting thorny issues individually is difficult as conflicts on these issues are messy and not easily resolved. Our human nature tells us to avoid such interactions. Too often, each party allows them to slide. This inaction often becomes the easy way for us to avoid the anxiety of a contentious conflict. We falsely hope that difficult issues will somehow sort themselves out without our interaction. Our flesh tells us to live in the comfortable world of denial or evasiveness that avoids confrontation on such issues. Regrettably, we discover that this illusionary world will eventually come crashing down on us as the penalty of inaction hits us. In effect, we allow our fear of confrontation to control us by allowing outside events to decide the issue. Usually, such decisions result in harsher consequences for us than if we had faced them earlier. The denying party usually feels the penalty harder, resulting in greater anger.

As the authors state in *Fighting for Your Marriage:* "But what we do know is that something important is at stake, you need to make a decision together, because decisions support a greater commitment to follow through on what has been decided. So where it matters, decide don't slide." Mutually facing these issues, using the principles set forth above, helps lead to a mutual resolution of the conflict. Both parties feel a part of the solution creating a greater sense of unity in the marriage. Even when we know these principles of positive conflict, we are challenged when our spouse doesn't agree with us.

Working as a team is critically important for a marriage or a relationship to succeed as there are so many things to do, especially when there are children. Such teamwork in getting the work done relieves stress in the marriage and thereby lowers the number and intensity of the conflicts. The relationship that works best is when you surprise your spouse by doing something beyond what is expected, like doing something your spouse usually does. Such unselfish giving is really a sign of love to the spouse or friend, which enhances the relationship.

A willingness to compromise. In a conflict over different ideas or plans, we need to learn to compromise on nonessential issues so that there is an opportunity for resolution. This definition of compromise is: "to adjust or settle by partial relinquishment of principles, position, or claims." Paul, in Acts, personifies his willingness to compromise to keep the peace in the Jerusalem Christian church. Members of that church had heard a false rumor that Paul was forbidding converted Jews from circumcising their children. To overcome this incorrect gossip, Paul joined four Jewish members of that church in participating and paying for all the men to purify themselves (Jewish purification requirements are in Numbers 6:9-20). In Acts 21:23-24, James, the brother of Jesus, and the elders of the Jerusalem church tell Paul: "'. . . *There are four men with us who have made a vow. Take these men and join in their purification rites and pay their expenses, so that they can have their heads shaved. Then everyone will know that there is no truth in these reports about you, but that you yourself are living in obedience to the law.'*" Note that Paul followed this request to bring peace to the church, but he did not renounce Jesus, or give up his Christian beliefs. We, too, must draw the line and never compromise our fundamental Christian beliefs. In Revelation 2:13, God addresses this: "'*I know where you live—where Satan is on the throne. Yet you remain true to my name. You did not renounce your faith in me, even in the days of Antipas, my faithful witness, who was put to death in your city—where Satan lives.*'" Standing firm in the face of adversity and suffering demonstrates the depth of our faith in Jesus. By doing this, we are often blessed by Him in some way.

Some people are so headstrong that they never want to compromise at all, even for the greater good of both parties. They selfishly stay fixed in their position, which often results in the other party feeling demeaned if they totally submit, so there is no resolution. When people remain stuck, they stop growing because they are not open to change(s) in their lives. Life becomes progressively harder as they are not able to adjust to life's changes so they often drop out by retreating into some addiction.

By working together the conflicting parties can seek creative solutions to their problems. While a win-win resolution might be preferable, it is not always achievable as some problems require only one solution. However, each party can have an attitude of evenhandedness that says: We'll do it your way this time but next time it will be my turn to decide.

Take responsibility to do your part in the marriage, or relationship. Each party in the marriage or in any relationship has a responsibility to help the relationship if it is to succeed. Becoming responsible in doing your part is a critical step in growing up for all of us. Rick Renner in his book, *Sparkling Gems from the Greek,* addresses responsibility: "There is only one reason weeds grow out of control in your garden— because no one took the proper time and care to uproot and remove them." Renner goes on: "His *lack of diligence* is the reason his garden got into this mess." Are you allowing your "garden," which stands for your life, become consumed by weeds? Paying attention to our responsibilities is important for the health and stability of all of our relationships.

Having perseverance when going through each of the above steps. Perseverance is defined as: "to press on despite opposition, resolute." Completing each of the above steps requires perseverance from both parties in order to become successful with positive conflict. Both parties will have a tendency to revert back to their old negative ways of conflict, as change is not always easy. In addition, each party may not change at the same rate. However, with both of our hearts resolved to find peace, we press on with these biblical mandates that enable us to find God's peace in our conflicts.

James speaks of the importance of perseverance in James 1:2-4: *"Consider it pure joy, my brothers, whenever you face trials of many kinds, because you know that the testing of your faith develops perseverance. Perseverance must finish its work so that you may be mature and complete, not lacking anything."* Conflict is a testing for both parties to see if they can resolutely pursue positive conflict. As we see from the verse from James, we need to pursue positive conflict to become mature with our conflicts and, thereby, achieve God's peace and greater intimacy in our lives.

We have seen that positive conflict is far better than the negative conflict types and styles that we have suffered under for most of our lives. The call now is to try using some of these positive conflict principles in a conflict. Remember that if the conflict starts to turn negative, stop and call a "time out" and pray for God's help to change the environment. He will eventually change the situation for the better. Also you can start a positive legacy by modeling this form of conflict to your children as they are watching you and thinking how to express themselves in a conflict.

Summary:

These principles of positive conflict in order of importance are:

Seeking God's help. It is critically important that we seek God's help through prayer and Bible reading (1 Corinthians 1:25).

Establishing a safe atmosphere for mutual communication. Safety is required in our conflicts if we feel free to express our opinions, or feelings (Proverbs 29:25 and Psalm 27:5). Use "carefronting" principles of care instead of confronting.

Showing respect:

> **Speak in a calm tone.** The initial tone of the speaker's voice sets the atmosphere for the conflict (Proverbs 15:1).

> **Use positive words.** Avoid harsh words about the person when correcting their behavior (Proverbs 12:18). Using "I" statements vs. "you" statements, which softens the harshness of the message.

> **Listen closely to the words spoken and the emotions shown.** Listen carefully enough so that you can repeat the exact words of the speaker—reflective listening (James 1:19).

> **Look the person in the eyes.** This natural means of connecting also allows you to be able to read their body language—shows their real intent.

Express your intentions clearly. This action reduces confusion. It requires us to think of the words that clearly express our desires before we speak them.

Face your conflict as a team. Don't let issues slide. Face them together to gain help and ideas to overcome any obstacles.

Be willing to compromise. We need to learn to compromise on nonessential things. Paul, in Acts 21:23-24.

Take responsibility to do your part in the marriage or relationship. Each party needs to feel a responsibility for the relationship, which is critical to maturing.

Have perseverance when going through each of the above steps. Completing each of the above steps requires perseverance from both parties to become successful with positive conflict.

Discussion Questions

1. What is the first principle of positive conflict?
Why is it so important?

2. What is "carefronting?" How is it different from confronting?

3. What are two of the four parts that comprise respect?
Are you using any of these in your conflicts?

4. How does compromise actually work in a conflict?

Epilogue

Bitterness is like a cancer that infects and destroys not only us, but can easily spread to all those around us including churches, communities and nations. Regrettably, those most affected by bitterness are our families and close friends. As I mentioned, I was a product of a broken family, so I know the pain that accompanies such a bitter breakup. If our attitudes are not corrected using the principles set forth in this book, bitterness will frequently cause a painful death to our closest relationships. Consequently, when the seeds of bitterness arise, we need to be alert to their danger and use intentional forgiveness and positive conflict to defeat them.

It is my hope that all people, Christian and non-Christian, will read and use this book to find release from their bitterness. Knowing what forgiveness is, and what it is not, helps us to understand it and how to use it effectively to overcome acrimony. It is critical to have a commitment to grant forgiveness to those who have hurt us and personally discover the freedom from the danger of a bitter heart.

Positive conflict provides an approach to better resolving our conflicts so that potential anger does not arise, or its subsequent relative, bitterness. The principles of positive conflict provide clear biblical principles that I, and others, have used effectively in reaching resolution.

It is my hope that buyers of this book will not only read the book themselves, but also use it in a small group. There, the opportunity for mutual discussion and personal revelation on this important topic can repair broken relationships. From my experience of using my first book, *Anger Reconciliation*, in a small group, I recommend this approach. I found that the group discussion opened many eyes of how to deal with their anger biblically. I will be writing an accompanying workbook on bitterness this winter as I did with my first book. The new workbook will be designed to help individuals seek help to overcome their bitterness. The people who have completed the first workbook tell me that they have grown in their personal understanding of anger and how to overcome it. I expect the same from this new workbook.

I pray that everyone reading this book will find a new hope for their relationships and, with God's help, achieve greater peace in their lives and more fulfilling personal relationships.

James Offutt
Spring 2012

You may contact me with your feedback, or a desire to order any of my books:

1. *Anger Reconciliation*

2. *Anger Reconciliation Workbook*

3. *From Bitterness to Reconciliation Workbook*
   (after January 2013).

I would appreciate hearing from you at:
Email: offutt2@hotmail.com
Website: angerispositive.com
Telephone: 315-395-4310

Notes

Chapter 1
What is Bitterness?

1. Rick Renner, *Sparkling Gems from the Greek* (Tulsa, OK, Teach All Nations 2003) p. 732.
2. Christopher Lane, Article in Psychology Today, May 28 entitled *Bitterness: The Next Disorder.*
3. Dr Les Carter, *The Anger Trap* (San Francisco, California, Jossey-Bass A Wiley Imprint 2003) p. 8.
4. Rick Renner, *Sparkling* p. 732.
5. Chip Ingram and Becca Johnson, *Overcoming Emotions that Destroy* (Grand Rapids, Michigan, BakerBooks a division of Baker Publishing 2009) p. 242.

Chapter 2
Roots of Bitterness

1. Renner, *Sparkling* p. 655.
2. Rober Schuller, *Leaning into God When Life is Pushing You Away* (New York, NY, FaithWorks a division of Hachette Book Group 2009) p. 52.
3. Ibid. p. 53.
4. Dwight L. Carlson, *"Overcoming Hurts and Anger"* (Eugene, Oregon, Harvest House, 1981) p. 151.
5. Schuller, *Leaning* p. 53.
6. Ingram, *Overcoming* p. 109.
7. Schuller, *Leaning* p. 118.
8. Ibid p.119.
9. Joni Eareckson Tada, *A Lifetime of Wisdom* (Grand Rapids Michigan, Zondervan 2009) p. 21.
10. Elizabeth Levang PhD, *When Men Grieve* (Minneapolis, Minn., Fairview Press 1998) p. 11.
11. Dr. Elizabeth Kubler-Ross, *On Death and Dying* (New York, NY., Macmillan Publishing Co., 1969) p. 179.

12. Ibid p. 4.

13. Levang, *When* p. 13.

Chapter 3
Biblical Examples of Bitterness and Other Characteristics

1. Chris Brauns, *Unpacking Forgiveness* (Wheaton, Illinois, Crossway Books, 2008) p. 154.

2. Gary Smalley and Ted Cunningham, *From Anger to Intimacy* (Ventura, California Regal from Gospel Light, 2009) p. 100.

3. Gary Oliver, *Real Men* (Chicago Illinois, Moody Press, 1993) p. 104.

4. Ingram, *Overcoming* p. 238.

5. Oliver, *Real* p. 110.

6. *An Independent Baptist Church* (www.gospelcenterchurch.org/bitterness).

Chapter 4
Stages One and Two of Bitterness

1. Ingram, *Overcoming* p. 244

2. Renner, *Sparkling* p. 985.

3. Chris Brauns, *Unpacking* p. 167.

4. Gary Chapman, *Anger: Handling a Powerful Emotion in a Healthy Way* (Chicago, Illinois, Northfield Publishing, 2007) p. 84.

Chapter 5
Stages Three and Four of Bitterness

1. Chapman, *Anger* p. 82.

2. Levang *When* p. 131 & 134.

3. Valery Satterwhite, *Resentment and Expectations: Big Fat Hold Ups* p 102.

4. Jim Wilson, *How to be Free from Bitterness* (Moscow, Idaho, Cannon Press and Community Christian Ministries, 2007 2nd edition) p. 9.

5. Gwen Mouliert, *Overcoming Bitterness,* (Mansfield. PA. Fire Wind, 2000) p. 124.

6. Ibid p. 49.

7. Erwin Lutzer, *When You've Been Wronged: Moving from Bitterness to Forgiveness,* (Chicago, Illinois, Moody Publishers, 2007) p. 29.

8. Ibid p. 37.

Chapter 6
Fear Leading to Bitterness

1. Thom Rutledge, *Embracing Fear and Finding the Courage to Live Your Life,* (New York, NY, HarperCollins, 2002) p. 5.

2. Jeff Golliher, *Moving Through Fear,* (New York, NY, Jeremy Tarcher a member of the Penguin Group USA, 2011) p. 12.

3. Rutledge, *Embracing* p. 1.

4. Golliher, *Moving* p. 32.

5. Oliver, *Real* p. 79.

6. Harold S. Kushner, *Conquering Fear,* (New York, NY, Alfred A. Knopf, 2009) p. 7-8.

7. Oliver, *Real* p. 81.

8. Golliher, *Moving* p. 20.

Chapter 7
Intentional Forgiveness Leading to Reconciliation

1. Lewis Smedes, *Forgive & Forget,* (New York, NY Pocket Books a division of Simon & Schuster, Inc.,1984) p. 91.

2. Smalley and Cunningham, *From Anger* p. 250.

3. Earnie Larsen, *From Anger to Forgiveness,* (New York, NY, A Kazeldon Foundation book, Ballantine Books, 1992) p. 123.

4. Smedes, *Forgive* p. 50.

5. Renner, *Sparkling* p. 775.

Chapter 8
Steps for Forgiveness

1. Jim Wilson, *How* p. 18.

2. Smalley and Cunningham, *From Anger* p. 138.

3. Smedes, *Forgive* p. 61.

4. Paul Meyer, *Forgiveness . . . the Ultimate Miracle,* (Orlando, Fl., Bridge-Logos, 2006) p. 35.

Chapter 9
Different Reactions by the Offender to Forgiveness
1. Lutzer, *When* p. 157.
2. Ibid. p. 158.
3. Smedes, *Forgive* p. 141.
4. Lutzer, *When* p. 155.

Chapter 10
Reconciliation with the Offender
1. Erwin Lutzer, *When* p.138-145.

Chapter 11
Conflict Patterns: Escalation and Avoidance
1. Carter, *The Anger Trap* p. 142.
2. Milan & Kay Yerkovich, *How We Love*, (Colorado Springs, CO, WaterBrook Press 2006) p. 6.
3. Tim Ursiny, *The Coward's Guide to Conflict,*(Naperville, Illinois, Sourcebooks Inc, 2003) p. 126.

Chapter 12
Conflict Patterns: Invalidation & Negative Interpretation
1. Roy Milam, article *Why Marriages Fail: Invalidation (Part 2 of 4)* (Cypress, TX, Cornerstone Marriage and Family Ministries) p. 1.
2. Kerby Anderson, article *Why Marriages Fail,"* (Richardson, TX, Probe Ministries International 1998) p. 3 & 4
3. Ibid. p.4.

Chapter 13
Conflict Pattern Styles
1. Bill Mitcham, article *Breaking Destructive Patterns Key to Couple Conflict Resolution* Mooresville Tribune, January 29, 2009).
2. Harriett Lerner, Phd, *The Dance of Anger*, (New York, NY, Harper & Row Publishers,1985) p. 58.
3. Ibid. p. 60.
4. Ibid p. 75.

5. Dr Les Carter, *The Anger Trap* p. 137.

Chapter 14
The Power of Positive Conflict

1. Howard Markman, Scott Stanley & Susan Blumberg, *Fighting for Your Marriage: Third Edition(* San Francisco, Cal. Jossey-Bass, 2010) p. 25.

2. Barbara Pachter, *The Power of Positive Confrontation,*(New York, NY, Marlowe & Company, 2000) p. 75.

3. Ibid. p. 74.

4. Markman, *Fighting* p. 96.

5. Renner, *Sparkling* p. 638.

CPSIA information can be obtained at www.ICGtesting.com
Printed in the USA
BVOW011303200912

300980BV00001B/4/P